D0448217

Growing Up Dead

Also by Peter Conners

Of Whiskey and Winter (poetry)

Emily Ate the Wind (novella)

Edited by Peter Conners

PP=FF: An Anthology

Growing Up DEAD

The HALLUCINATED CONFESSIONS of a TEENAGE DEADHEAD

Peter Conners

WITHDRAWN

DA CAPO PRESS

A Member of the Perseus Books Group

Copyright© 2009 by Peter Conners
Lyrics to Grateful Dead songs, copyright Ice Nine
Publishing Company. Used with Permission.
"Deadhead Detectives Have Lots of Tickets," *Albany
Times Union*, March 28, 1993.
Used By Permission, Times Union, Albany, NY.

All rights reserved. No part of this publication may be
reproduced, stored in a retrieval system, or transmitted,
in any form or by any means, electronic, mechanical,
photocopying, recording, or otherwise, without the prior
written permission of the publisher. Printed in the
United States of America. For information, address Da
Capo Press, 11 Cambridge Center, Cambridge, MA 02142.

Set in 10.5 point Mercury Text G1 by The Perseus Books Group

Cataloging-in-Publication data for this book is available
from the Library of Congress.
ISBN-13: 978-0-306-81733-5

Published by Da Capo Press
A Member of the Perseus Books Group
www.dacapopress.com

Da Capo Press books are available at special discounts for
bulk purchases in the U.S. by corporations, institutions,
and other organizations. For more information, please
contact the Special Markets Department at the Perseus
Books Group, 2300 Chestnut Street, Suite 200,
Philadelphia, PA 19103, or call (800) 810-4145, ext. 5000,
or e-mail special.markets@perseusbooks.com.

10 9 8 7 6 5 4 3 2 1

For everyone who got on the bus.

I think of the Grateful Dead as being a crossroads or a pointer sign and what we're pointing to is that there's a lot of universe available, that there's a whole lot of experience available over here.

—JERRY GARCIA, 1970

CONTENTS

VIII

CONTENTS

Introduction
(Tuning Up)

Let's put it this way: the high point of the song "Truckin'"—and one of the Dead's most recognizable lyrics—isn't "What a long strange trip it's been" for nothing. Throughout my touring life, different friends and Deadheads dropped into and out of the scene, but the core family I toured with just kept *trucking on*. That core family is who I kept in mind while writing this book. It is our story I am trying to tell. In a way, it is the fulfillment of a promise I have been making to them— wherever they are—for twenty years. As I spoke to different people while researching this book, I was always amazed at the names and cities that popped up.

Shasta and Sissy in particular were invaluable in reminding me of places we had been, who was there, what happened, and helping me rekindle the energy of our touring years. I thank everyone else who helped jog my memory as well. Those touring years get mighty fuzzy. For example, I honestly can't remember ever seeing the Dead at Landover, Maryland, much less seeing them there during different runs. But, as it turns out, that story was verified by multiple sources. I find those revelations sort of funny, vexing, disconcerting, but ultimately accurate to how I "remember" the overall act of touring. It wasn't about the specifics of where and when, it was about being on the road, on the bus. Everything and everyone you came across in the larger tapestry of that world bled into the overall experience of being on tour. In my tour life, there was the solid core of our family, but there were also dozens of friends and Deadheads who we hooked up with for anywhere from one show to a whole tour and then lost touch of completely. That was the nature of the scene. One day you're pooling money so everyone can have a few bites of stir fry before the show, the next you're trying to remember who the hell that girl was who made off with your Brent shirt (it was Sally, and I'll never forgive her for it).

The Pulitzer Prize–winning poet W. D. Snodgrass wrote, "How could one be a first-rate artist without offending, deeply, those he most loves?" I don't know what rate we're working with here, but I beg Shasta, Sissy, and everyone else who will recognize themselves in this book, for their indulgence as I try to piece together the shards of our collective past.

Despite wonderful stories of eight-hour shows in the 1960s and 1970s, Dead shows during my touring heyday tended to last about two hours. However, being a Deadhead is not a two-hour experience. Being a Deadhead is a way of life. Thus, many of the stories in this book revolve around becoming and living as a Deadhead outside the Grateful Dead concert. Blasphemously, I would equate that viewpoint to someone who claims that religion shapes all of their thinking, even outside of the physical confines of their church, synagogue, mosque, etc. For many Deadheads, being at a Dead show was a religious experience, and the resonances of that experience touched everything they did before and after the show. We were certainly pilgrims for the Dead. However, for every person, the feeling, the rationale, the path of finding and living the life of a Deadhead is different.

This is mine.

One common reaction I received when I told people I was writing a book about being a Deadhead was, essentially, "Aren't Deadheads just a bunch of middle-class white

kids?" This reaction was usually coupled with a dis-
dain for what the observer considered Deadhead
phoniness: why would a bunch of middle-class white
kids want to "act poor" (an actual quote) and scrounge
around the country in crappy cars and even crappier
clothes? This response is only natural. We all—myself
included—love stories about people who overcome
economic, physical, or mental challenges to "better"
themselves. To overcome. To make it big, succeed, and
get ahead. And in these people's eyes, Deadheads do
none of those things. If anything, Deadheads take the
natural advantages they are born with in this culture—
skin color, wealth, education, etc.—and spit on them.
Or worse, ignore them completely. These observations
are echoed by sociologist Rebecca G. Adams, who says,
"The cultural mainstream applies a tribal stigma to
Deadheads because they do not appear to be what they
should be."

As I encountered these biases more and more, it
became obvious to me that Deadhead-haters (and there
are plenty of them) often saw Deadheads' motives as a
rejection of core value systems. Which, of course,
quickly translates to a perceived rejection of the
individual's value system. And, in turn, a rejection of
that person. As Adams pointed out, stigma against
Deadheads is particularly strong because membership is
voluntary. "When participation and identity is voluntary,

as with the Deadhead community, the idea is that people who do not want to experience stigma can simply end or hide their affiliation. It is thus fair to expect that the stigma assigned to Deadheads who choose to make their membership in the community known to others is relatively potent."

Apparently, our late 20th-century glorification of the lovable slacker—including nationwide hysteria over the "dumbing down" of American culture—has been deleted like so much spam (the annoying e-version, not the gelatinous slacker delicacy). In one sense, we can thank Bart Simpson for the editorial fodder that established popular culture studies programs across academia, thus creating dozens of classes that are excellent to attend while totally baked. In another, we can curse academia for sucking all the dumb fun out of popular culture.

When everything means something, mindless fun loses its Zen-like pizzazz.

Ironically enough, the term "hippie" (often erroneously synonymous with "Deadhead") derived from the beatnik word "hip," which essentially meant you were cool. You "understood" what was going on in an intuitive way. You knew the score. You weren't trying too hard to do anything at all. You just *were*.

Hippies were the children of the Beatniks.

Now here I must admit my grudging, but functional, use of the term *beatnik*. This, as Allen Ginsberg called it, "foul term" was coined by Herb Caen in an April 2, 1958, article in the *San Francisco Chronicle*. It was intended—and succeeded—as a put-down. Caen's article was published roughly six months after the launch of Russia's Sputnik satellite. It appeared in the thick of the San Francisco Poetry Renaissance that saw the Beat authors devolve rapidly from underground icons to media-scarred cultural stereotypes. By mixing Jack Kerouac's self-generated label "Beat" with America's paranoia over Communist supremacy via the phallic-shot heard 'round the world, Caen succeeded in demonizing an entire generation of pacifist, poetry-reading, philosophy-spewing, chess-playing, coffee shop–sitting, middle-class white kids as a threat to American values.

By the time Caen's article appeared, Jack Kerouac's *On the Road* had already been published to a wide range of reviews. *On the Road* may have launched a thousand horrible open mic poetry readings, but the book and Beat literature in general was seminal in the life of the Grateful Dead. As Jerry Garcia said in his October 1991 *Rolling Stone* interview (for which he appeared on the cover of the magazine): "I owe a lot of who I am and what I've been and what I've done to the beatniks from the Fifties and to the poetry and art and music that I've come in contact with. I feel like I'm part of a continuous line of a certain thing in American culture, a root." Although hindsight consideration of

On the Road focuses on Kerouac's melancholia, misogyny, or religiosity, upon its publication the book was regarded as a celebration of restless, post–World War II youth. In his admirably insightful review published in the *New York Times* on September 5, 1957, Gilbert Millstein said that the publication of *On the Road* was "a historic occasion" and declared it "the most beautifully executed, the clearest and the most important utterance yet made by the generation Kerouac himself named years ago as 'beat.' . . . "

Lest we forget, *On the Road* was also a celebration of good, dumb fun. Or, as Kerouac called them, "kicks."

By the time Caen's article appeared, Allen Ginsberg and City Lights Books had also won an obscenity trial that sought to ban the distribution of Ginsberg's watershed poem, *Howl*. This poem—also a major touchstone for the Dead—is now accepted as one of most relevant and socially significant poems ever written by an American. It's hard to believe that publisher, poet, and bookstore owner Lawrence Ferlinghetti was arrested and that copies of the book were confiscated by customs officials who stated, "You wouldn't want your children to come across it."

Considering that in the late 1980s, the Federal Communications Commission ruled that any station airing the complete *Howl* could be fined for broadcasting indecent material, sometimes it's hard to remember that he won.

In any event, the war between the straight and the cool was on, and the cool were winning. It was time for the establishment—the guardians of American values—to strike back. The future of the country—an entire generation of kids who could be lost to the romantic notion of wandering highways, spewing poetry at the clouds, and doing nothing to assure America's economic and militaristic dominance in the world—was at stake.

Unfortunately, no sooner had the Beats become the oft-mocked and even scorned Beatniks than the entire scene grew their hair out and became hippies. Tinny bongos were replaced by distorted electric guitars. In place of coffee and the occasional hit of "tea" there was LSD and lots and lots of "tea." In place of hushed, private debates over philosophy, there were raucous political rallies that publicly shook the political establishment to its wingtips. The rift between the hippies and the straights was larger than Caen, Kerouac, or anyone on either side could have predicted.

And whenever there is a rift, there is a natural urge to demonize those on the other side. Otherwise, how do you know which side you're on?

So to all the Deadhead-haters out there who sneer, "Aren't Deadheads just a bunch of middle-class white kids?" my answer, is yes, that sums up a fair portion of the crowd. But so what? Deadheads aren't just hippies or Beats. But just like many of the hippies and Beats who have stood up for all the ideals that we claim as defining American characteristics—freedom of religion, expression, civil rights, women's rights, and the celebration of individuality at all its levels—yes, many Deadheads are middle-class (acknowledging a huge economic range within that term as well) white kids. But not all Deadheads are alike. In fact, not all Deadheads are cool. Actually, many are pretty uptight. And in the case of Al Gore, some Deadheads are simultaneously cool *and* uptight.

It should also be acknowledged that Deadheads—middle-class and white as they may be—are also the final manifestation of a certain alternative culture right before it splintered into a million—often market-driven, media-generated—factions. Deadheads are the last bastions of the old-guard American resistance to consumer culture and all that it entails. At a certain point, Madison Avenue recognized that the war between straight and cool could be repackaged as a generation Gap (with a capital G) and sold back to kids who never realized it already belonged to them. Yet somehow, marketers outside the Dead community have never quite figured out how to co-opt Deadhead culture. Kurt Cobain may have despised Deadheads, but in the end, he might've envied their relative anonymity as well. Fans may have hounded Jerry, but the media seldom did.

Jerry may have worn flannel shirts before Kurt, but no store ever sold a kid a flannel with the promise it would make him look more like Jerry.

The earliest incarnation of the group that would become the Grateful Dead was a raggedy collection of folk and blues enthusiasts and wild-eyed high school kids calling themselves Mother McCree's Uptown Jug Champions. The winking "Champions" part aside, this was not an ironical name. Mother McCree's Uptown Jug Champions actually played jug band music. A review of the band's members and their instruments will prove this. The band consisted of Jerry Garcia (guitar), Bob Weir (washtub bass and jug), Tom Stone (banjo), Dave Parker (washboard), and Ron "Pigpen" McKernan (harmonica).

Interestingly enough, many of the songs covered by Mother McCree's stayed in the Dead's repertoire for years ("Viola Lee Blues," "Good Morning Little School Girl," "Monkey and the Engineer"). Some they played for the entire life of the band ("Minglewood Blues," "Little Red Rooster," and, sporadically, "Big Boss Man").

Still, Mother McCree's was not built for the long haul. Although the folk purist Garcia and the blues aficionado Pigpen held out for as long as they could, the Beatles' fabled appearance on the *Ed Sullivan Show* on February

9, 1964, unalterably changed America's musical tastes. The rest of the British Invasion—including Pigpen's beloved Rolling Stones—drove the point home with all the subtlety of a railroad spike to the temple. The zeitgeist doors had been thrown open; the frenetic energy of rock-n-roll youth was unleashed. By the end of 1964, the idea of washboard-driven songs would seem as quaint and outdated as a ripping lute solo in the middle of "Jailhouse Rock."

The next incarnation of the band—fully electrified— showed up as The Warlocks. The addition of avant-garde composer prodigy Phil Lesh helped push the boys into deeper, stranger territories. The rest of the band consisted of Garcia, Weir, Pigpen, and the best drummer in their Palo Alto neighborhood, Bill Kreutzman. The band played their first two gigs at a place called Magoo's Pizza Parlor in Menlo Park, California, on May 5 and May 12 of 1965. (Again, the name of this establishment was not ironic. It was, in actuality, a pizza parlor.) Lesh didn't actually join the band until their third gig. However, he was in attendance—high on acid—at the second one. Apparently he was impressed enough that when Garcia slid into Lesh's booth during set break and offered/insisted "Listen, man, you're gonna play bass in my band," Lesh accepted. From then on, the crucial intellectual engagement between Phil and Jerry would drive the band forward with improvisational influences ranging from the avant-garde composer Luciano Berio to blind bluesman Reverend Gary Davis to the Beats to Ornette Coleman to Lenny Bruce and well beyond informing their aesthetic.

As fate would have it, the name The Warlocks was already taken by at least two other recording acts at that time, including a Texas band that would later emerge as ZZ Top. The Warlocks needed a new name. The story goes that the Grateful Dead was named after Jerry Garcia came upon the term while leafing through a Funk and Wagnall's dictionary. In his own words, "Everything else on the page went blank, diffuse, just sorta oozed away, and there was GRATEFUL DEAD, *big* black letters *edged* all around in gold, man, blasting out at me, such a stunning combination." The term *Grateful Dead* was coined by nineteenth-century musicologist Francis Child as a way to refer to a classic ballad or folktale plotline. In these tales, a character would come across a corpse that couldn't be properly buried because the person had died in debt. The character, out of pure human kindness, would settle the corpse's debt and pay for the burial. In turn, the spirit of the corpse would emerge at some point down the road to help the character when he was in need.

In other words, it is a beautiful karmic tale.

Although not all the band members were sold on the name (it *was* sort of creepy, after all), the name stuck.

With the 1967 addition of Bill's new friend, drummer Mickey Hart, the band had struck on its original core lineup. The Grateful Dead were born.

Twenty years later, I would climb "on the bus" to go to my first Dead show.

CHAPTER ONE

Kingswood Music Theatre, June 30, 1987

Set 1: *Touch of Grey, Greatest Story Ever Told, Loser, New Minglewood Blues, Candyman, Far From Me, Mama Tried, Big River, Ramble on Rose, When I Paint My Masterpiece, Don't Ease Me In*

Set 2: *Scarlet Begonias > Fire on the Mountain > Scarlet Begonias, Estimated Prophet > Eyes of the World > Jam > Drums > Space > Spanish Jam > The Other One > China Doll > Dear Mr. Fantasy > Around and Around > Good Lovin'*

Encore: *Box of Rain*

I was sixteen years old and had crossed the border in an orange van with three other kids from my high school—Bart, Beaker, and Ron—our bags of pot stuffed into various rusty crevices around the shitty shell of the van and six hits of pink dove LSD in my wallet. It was my first Grateful Dead show. The band was playing the amphitheater in Canada's Wonderland Amusement Park. We had driven to the show from my suburb of Pittsford, NY, that afternoon and rolled into the parking lot three hours before showtime. I had failed math again that year. I was supposed to be back in Pittsford in time for summer school the next morning at 8 A.M.

Ron's first show was the Dead in Buffalo, NY, 1986, with Tom Petty opening. A few of my friends had seen that show, but aside from some random stories that had to do with eating LSD-dosed sugar cubes and getting lost on the vast floor of Rich Stadium, they hadn't brought back many stories about the band. Most of my friends had already been tripping on acid pretty regularly since 10th grade. At that time, Bart was the only friend I knew who had seen a show earlier than 1986—Rochester War Memorial, 11/08/85—the second of a two-night stand, a smoking show with a rare cover of The Beatles' "Revolution" to open the second set.

It was Beaker's van. None of us had really hung out with Beaker before going up to Canada together. He was an oddball, a science geek with huge thick glasses and a raging, greasy Afro. He took all the advanced classes, which is why we seldom crossed paths. His lanky body seemed made from scrap parts of other bodies—as if the monster had created Dr. Frankenstein instead of vice versa—and he mumbled every word in the way of someone who always knew the right answer in class, but also knew the social danger in being the kid who knew every answer. He was physically awkward; unattractive; and unknowably, scientifically smarter than anyone else in the class. Aside from this show, my only memory of Beaker is the time he had a party while his parents were out of town. I've never seen a nice suburban house treated so horribly. Teenagers kicked holes into the walls of their living room. The two white columns framing their front door were demolished. Family photographs were crudely doodled on with magic marker. Their possessions (plates, jewelry, records, furniture, you name it) were stolen, destroyed, or otherwise desecrated. I personally puked off a monster bong hit in Beaker's bedroom (Beaker wasn't in there at the time, just me and a bunch of my friends who all scattered after I puked. I recovered, wiped my mouth, finished the bong hit, drank all their beers, and then went to see what else was going on at the party). Beaker's party ended in a massive fistfight in the front yard between kids from my high school and kids who had crashed the party from another school. That finally drove the neighbors to call the cops. I have no idea what took them so long. The next day the neighbors found someone's teeth—apparently the kids who'd lost the fight—in their driveway.

Prior to touring with the Dead, I had limited experience with vans. When I was nine years old, I had a friend named David whose family moved to Rochester from California for a couple of years and then left. His parents listened to Fleetwood Mac and ate dinners comprised solely of vegetables, which was something I had never seen before. They used beanbag chairs as if they were actual furniture. His father had a thick mustache and his mother wore loose, floppy shirts with embroidered flowers around the neck and sleeves. They drove a blue Ford van. Prior to going to Dead shows, I had probably been in three vans my entire life. After that, it wasn't uncommon for me to spend an entire summer living in one.

Ron and I had been friends since we were little kids. When we were still in elementary school, his family used to take me with them to Martha's Vineyard for two weeks in the summer. We did the usual stuff: fishing, swimming, body surfing, eating ice cream, playing lazily, and then complaining we were bored. It was truly idyllic. But in retrospect I really have only one strong memory of those summer trips: going to the Flying Horses Carousel on Oak Bluffs. I don't know why this stands out to me so much. Granted, it was an old carousel, built in 1876, and I'm sure the horses were beautiful and historic and special, but that wouldn't have meant much to me then, and still doesn't today. I think that my memory of the Flying Horses Carousel is built on two foundations. One, going there was a tradition in Ron's family. They made a big deal out of it, so I figured it was a big deal, and even now I attach more importance to it than it deserves. And two, this was the kind of carousel where you try to grab a brass ring as you go around. On each revolution you reached over to this machine that dispensed the rings, and if you got there and there was a brass ring, you grabbed it—naturally—and Bingo! you had grabbed the brass ring. Free ride, I guess, but really—who cared?

But since "reaching for the brass ring" is an expression people still use, when they say this silly and cliché thing I have a personal memory to attach to it. I have reached for the brass ring. Perhaps I even got it a few times.

But more important—and here's how the Dead either works for you or doesn't—there is a Dead song called "Crazy Fingers" with these lyrics:

> *Midnight on a carousel ride*
> *Reaching for the gold ring*
> *Down inside*
> *Never could reach it*
> *It just slips away*
> *But I try*

And when I heard those lyrics in the middle of that song it touched me on a level that was so profoundly personal that it burrowed immediately down to the level of subconscious childhood memories. I didn't hear those lyrics and think about them in any quotidian sense. When I was dancing in a summer field surrounded by thousands of Deadheads and Jerry Garcia peeled off those shimmering lines, they merged memories from my childhood with the intensely powerful communal experience I was having and flash-soldered my inner and outer worlds. It was intense exaltation. I was, at once, a bewildered child and a new adult tasting more freedom than I'd ever known. I was a freak by choice, wearing torn cutoff jean shorts, tossing my long, knotty mane; I was dancing, grooving, making my body do things it had never done; all around me people were lost in their own reveries, freaking out, trembling in fear, blissful, writhing, sometimes flat-out fucking; and with those few lyrics Jerry introduced my old world to my new world and they hugged, held each other, laughing, crying, exultant. . . .

I am a Generation Xer. I use irony and cynicism the way my parents used tennis and business conversation: as a way to understand the world and relate to their peers. But I cannot be cynical about what happened to me between 1987 and 1992 at Grateful Dead concerts all across the United States. The experiences that I had on tour with the Grateful Dead were among the most powerful of my life and, in many profound ways, made me who I am today. And who is that? No one in particular. But here's the thing: when I walked out of Kingswood Music Theatre in 1987, I had been profoundly changed by what I'd just experienced. I would spend the next five years of my life focused intensely on doing whatever it took to attend Grateful Dead shows. As a result, I just barely passed high school and then dropped out of college, sold drugs, slept out on the street, smoked pounds of pot, ate enough LSD to power San Francisco for an entire weekend, and lived within a portable reality that shaped every space it encountered rather than vice versa.

I had become a Deadhead.

I will always be a Deadhead.

According to the website HistoryCentral.com, the most popular songs of 1987 are as follows:

1) "Open Your Heart" by Madonna
2) "Livin' on a Prayer" by Bon Jovi
3) "Jacob's Ladder" by Huey Lewis and the News
4) "Lean on Me" by Club Nouveau
5) "Nothing's Going to Stop Us Now" by Starship

6) "I Knew You Were Waiting" by Aretha Franklin
and George Michael
7) "Died in Your Arms" by Cutting Crew
8) "With or Without You" by U2
9) "You Keep Me Hanging On" by Kim Wilde
10) "Always" by Atlantic Starr

Allow me to add to this list the following bands who received heavy airplay during the 1980s: Loverboy, A Flock of Seagulls, Night Ranger, Wang Chung, Tommy Tutone, Men at Work, Journey, Bananarama, Toto, Kajagoogoo, Pet Shop Boys, Oingo Boingo, Stryper, Milli Vanilli, White Snake, and New Kids on the Block. Go back and listen to them. This music has not aged well. I realize that 1980s bands and their synthesized sounds go in and out of fashion and will always have fierce defenders who consider the decade to be a golden age of pop. But, lest we forget, when this music was being produced in the 1980s, it was being created as a pure product. In the early 1970s, John Chowning, an avant-garde composer and Stanford professor, discovered that by manipulating computer sine waves he could simulate the sounds of different instruments. This procedure became known as FM (frequency modulation) synthesis. In 1983, Yamaha introduced their DX9 and DX7 synthe-sizers, which included Chowning's FM technology, and—bang—the sounds of the 80s were born. As cool as the technology was in theory, it got leaned on too heavily and soon burned out the ears of listeners hungry for more natural sounds. In the 1980s, for every U2 there were fifteen Animotions. And remember, there was no irony in these bands. No smirk. It wasn't yet retro. Boys wore parachute pants and casual headbands. Girls wore legwarmers, even in the summer, and haircuts that poofed out in front like those Blooming Onions you eat at outdoor festivals. These 80s bands were exploring a new, synthesized frontier that quickly grew painful, and if anything, their sincerity, their lack of self-aware irony, was palpably, disturbingly real.

Now I'm not saying there wasn't decent music being made in the 1980s. Because there was. Lots of it. But I can say that very little of it reached my suburb of Pittsford, NY. And when it did reach us—like listening to the Sex Pistols' 1977 album *Anarchy in the U.K.* at fourteen years old in my friend's basement—I had no context in which to hear it. Thus no real idea of what I was listening to. To me, the Sex Pistols just looked funny and sounded like a bunch of guys who couldn't play or sing. I didn't gain any real appreciation of punk music until I was in my twenties and read Greil Marcus' *Lipstick Traces: A Secret History of the 20th Century.* Marcus helped me see the relevance, the importance of the fact that the Sex Pistols were guys who looked funny and couldn't play or sing. The Sex Pistols were a band burning alive in poverty and rebellion at the end of the world. But at fourteen, I had no idea what the Sex Pistols or, really, any nonmainstream contemporary bands were all about. The suburbs are not exactly a breeding ground for the contemplation of urban social unrest. The Talking Heads made more sense to a kid in the suburbs ("this is not my beautiful house, this is not my beautiful wife"), but even they were barely a blip on my admittedly provincial aural radar screen.

So when my friends and I started getting into music in high school, we never thought to focus on the music that was currently being made. We thought the stuff they were playing on the radio was shit and didn't come across any other new music that turned us on. Don't get me wrong, I can still sing you the lyrics to dozens of popular 80s songs. Plus, MTV started when I was ten years old, so—although my parents didn't get cable at their house until after I graduated from college, leaving me mooching off friends or waiting for Friday Night Videos—we tended to watch ridiculous videos of the same shitty music we heard constantly on the radio. We didn't just hear Kajagoogoo. We were assaulted with Kajagoogoo. So, in response, once we started to gain some independence—to hang out together outside our parents' houses, to drive, drink, hook up with girls, smoke cigarettes and pot, and basically form our teenage identities—my friends and I dipped back into music that happened before video, before all the bullshit we heard on the radio, before Jefferson Airplane had morphed into Starship and "We Built This City." We listened to music from the 1960s: The Doors, Led Zeppelin, Pink Floyd, Creedence Clearwater Revival, the Grateful Dead. . . . This wasn't just music, it was mythology. These bands and the men who represented them—Jim Morrison, Robert Plant, Jimmy Page, Syd Barrett, Jerry Garcia—came complete with vivid, epic stories and legacies. There weren't slick videos of these guys chasing tiger girls through the jungles of Rio (Duran Duran) or dancing with midgets in some trashy Renaissance seaport (Culture Club). Instead, there were still photos of them getting arrested during concerts. Photos of them sweaty, holding guitars on stage in front of thousands of screaming fans and completely lost in the music they were playing. They were dressed in leather jackets and pants. Or better yet, ponchos. They were smothered by groupies. These guys were different, weird, and, most important, they made the music themselves. That might sound funny, but it's an important enough concept to repeat: they made the music themselves. Watching videos during the heyday of MTV was enough to make you think that musicians were just people who danced and sang while computer programs churned out anonymous new hits in the background.

Jimi Hendrix might've gotten showy at times (as he himself admitted)—playing behind his back, with his teeth, torching his guitars, all gimmicks he came to despise—but he always really played. In other words, to a kid growing up in the 1980s suburbs, these bands from the 1960s seemed real. And listening to their music, hearing stories about their wild behavior, staring for hours at still photos of them in action, made me feel real. Authentic, if you will, in an era when authenticity was hard to come by.

On September 26, 1987, the Grateful Dead's song "Touch of Grey," off their album *In the Dark*, reached #9 on the *Billboard* singles chart. In a thirty-year career, it was their only song to ever reach the top twenty. The Dead also filmed a video for "Touch of Grey" that received regular airplay on MTV. It was filmed at Laguna Seca Raceway in California and shows the band playing the song as skeleton puppets until the very end, when they turn into the actual band members. There is a shot of a pretty, short-haired blond girl riding someone's shoulders and waving her arms in the crowd. That girl graduated from my high school two years before me. Which is all to say, just around the time I went from being a Grateful Dead fan to becoming a full-blown Deadhead, it became more fashionable to like the Grateful Dead. So, of course, Deadheads who had been around for a while resented any new fans who came on the scene after "Touch of Grey" reached the charts. They even had a name for them: touches.

This prejudice is as natural as it is ridiculous.

Nevertheless, let the record show that I attended my first Dead show 58 days before "Touch of Grey" hit the top ten.

Not only was Kingswood Music Theatre my first Dead show, it was only the second proper concert—of any band—that I had ever seen. My first was Peter Gabriel on November 7, 1986, at the Rochester War Memorial (renamed the Blue Cross Arena at the War Memorial in 1998 in solemn honor of all the money Blue Cross forked over for badly needed renovations). It was the first show of his *This Way Up Tour,* but I really didn't know much about Peter Gabriel outside of his well-played repertoire ("Solsbury Hill," "In Your Eyes," "Biko," "Don't Give Up," etc.). So aside from it being my first concert, it wasn't all that meaningful. Mainly, at that time, my friends and I were into drinking beer as fast as we could through an enormous red funnel attached to three feet of clear plastic tubing. In fact, we were so into it that we managed to get our hands on a funnel that held fourteen beers. To properly drink out of a fourteen-beer funnel you need one person to hold up the funnel, one person to hold the tube and help steady the funnel once it gets past the six-pack mark, one person to open and pour beers, and a few more guys to grow agitated and make loud noises as the funnel fills up and then to drink it.

My friends and I rolled into the parking lot for that concert and immediately started working through the couple cases of Budweiser my oldest-looking friend, Corey, had managed to buy over the counter with a fake I.D. from an Italian deli in a neighboring town. As you might expect, it doesn't take a pack of teenagers long to drink a couple cases of beer through a fourteen-beer funnel. In fact, it happens dangerously fast. Strangely enough, one of the overriding memories I have of that concert was the tameness of the crowd in the parking lot. It's not as if it was a Dio concert where excessive beer drinking would've most certainly drawn devil horns of approval. No, this was Peter Gabriel. As it stood, it was pretty much just a bunch of us suburban kids transplanted to a downtown parking lot drinking as much beer as we could as fast as we could before the concert started. Apparently we were under the impression that this would enhance our concert-going experience. Following that vein of logic, I might also mention here two other related rituals from this funnel phase: 1) spitting into the communal funnel, whereby each person about to do a funnel must spit into the funnel and then everyone drinks each other's spit along with the beer; 2) puking for distance, whereby funneling of said beer causes projectile vomiting, which is always more fun when done beside a good friend, who, when necessary, if he is not yet ready to vomit but you are, is willing to drink really fast to make sure that he can vomit next to you so you don't have to vomit alone.

Both are essential bonding experiences that I am thrilled to never have to do, or witness, again.

Although it wasn't focused on beer drinking, the partying in the parking lot of Kingswood Music Theatre was definitely sanctioned by the crowd. Anyone who ever went to a Dead show (or even just heard about it) can attest to the fact that the parking lot was an important part of the overall experience. Even that term, Dead *show*, illustrates the importance of the crowd. You would have never heard Deadheads calling a concert a concert, e.g., "Did you go to Greensboro? Killer concert!" Never. That phrasing would have been completely suspect. Instead it was, "Did you go to Greensboro? Killer show!" And, let's face it: the Grateful Dead did not put on a "show" as most people in show business, any form of show business at all, know it. There were no pyrotechnics (aside from the 1974 five-night run of Winterland shows when—as seen in the excellent *The Grateful Dead Movie*—a crazy-ass bastard named Boots sets off fireballs beside Keith's piano), no cage dancers, no absurdly oversized stage props—phallic or otherwise—and the band themselves rarely moved more than three feet in either direction, and, even then, only to take a drag off a cigarette (Garcia), or adjust their rigs (most likely Weir). Not to put too fine a point on it, but Jerry so much as swaying back and forth in time to what he was playing was the equivalent of a Pete Townshend windmill: the crowd went nuts, a crescendo had been reached, and Deadheads would giddily recount to each other his every sway. So referring to a Dead concert as a *show* certainly had little to do with the band members or their stage show. No, a Dead *concert* was a Dead *show* because Deadheads made it into one. And the show started well before the band ever took the stage. It started in the parking lot.

In contrast to the suburb we all lived in, Beaker's shitty van did not look out of place in the parking lot of Kingswood Music Theatre. In fact, shitty vans were the norm. Of course, the penultimate Deadhead vehicle will always be the Volkswagen camper. I'm not really sure how the VW camper became so closely associated with Dead culture, but, as with many Dead-head traditions, it was most likely pure, albeit relative, common sense. VW campers were cheap, used ones could be found everywhere, they weren't bad on gas considering their size, and they were specifically made for traveling and sleeping in for extended periods of time. Another common vehicle in Dead show parking

lots was the self-modified van. People would take
regular Econolines or similar basic Ford or Chevy vans
and trick them out for camping—they'd cut holes in
the roof; add a "widow's walk" for people to stand up
in; build in stoves, beds, storage space, and bike racks;
and, of course, give them a funky, trippy paint job and
cover them in Dead stickers. So as Beaker's van pulled
into the Kingswood parking lot, we felt right at home:
he had a Steal Your Face sticker on the back window
(stickers are massively important in Deadhead culture
and will be addressed more thoroughly later in the
book), a weird orange paint job that he'd done
himself, and he'd even cut a hole in the roof in a
shoddy attempt to install a Plexiglass moonroof.

One of the first things that struck me upon pulling
into Kingswood was the people we didn't know ran-
domly smiling, waving, and welcoming us in as we
slowly navigated the lot looking for a parking space.
These people didn't work for the venue, nor did they
work for the band. They were just people. Deadheads.
And they were happy to see that we had made it safely to
the show. I specifically remember asking the wiser, more
experienced Bart who these people were and his
response coming back: Rainbow people.

And he was right. They *were* Rainbow people.

The Rainbow Family of Living Light is, according to
one clever website, "the largest non-organization of

non-members in the world." The Family is most closely associated with events called Rainbow Gatherings, which are held in national forests every year. To imagine a Rainbow Gathering you can basically roll together every stereotypical image you have of a 1960s hippie commune, transplant it to modern day, and shift it nomadically around the country. Many people who go to Rainbow Gatherings go by Rainbow names usually derived from nature (Tree, Plant, Stone, Creek, etc.), animals (Bear, Puma, Deer, Coyote, etc.), the elements (Earth, Air, Fire, Water), or sometimes from the places where they attended their first Gathering (Modac, Tapoca, etc.). Events and activities happen at Rainbow Gatherings, but no one is in charge of them. Communal food is cooked, served, and cleaned up after on a volunteer basis, and, again, no one is officially in charge. Ditto parking, the first aid center (called by the acronym CALM for the Center for Alternative Living Medicine), the council meetings, sweat lodges, trade circles, info center, scouting council, and so on. The idea, of course, is that—unlike everywhere else humans have congregated from time immemorial—there is no hierarchy at a Rainbow Gathering. So, yes, Rainbow Gatherings are a lovely idea. Many of the Family's values (sorry) derive from Native American principles of respecting and living in harmony with the Earth. Who can argue with that? And my first impression of Rainbow people was most favorable. Here they were in the parking lot at Kingswood, the most fully hippied-out people I had ever seen, welcoming us, complete strangers and neophyte Dead fans, to the show.

We piled out of the van in various states of stoned disarray. The pink dove LSD was on our tongues just before we had crossed the border, so we were all starting to feel that tingle swim through our systems. Personally, I always felt LSD in my stomach first—or, more accurately, in the navel region—which, according to Taoist tenets that I encountered years later, is as it should be. The Navel Chakra or Shen Ch'ue (translated as "Mind Palace") is considered by Taoists to be the central holding chamber of one's ch'i-energy. According to them, the Shen Ch'ue gathers, assimilates, balances, and disseminates energy from both the outside world, including the external environment and everyone in it, and the internal energy from one's own bodily organs and state of mind. They trace the importance of this central spot back to our first worldly physical attachment—the umbilical cord in the womb—and say that the Navel Chakra represents our strongest connecting link to people, and to our own bodies, throughout our entire lives.

What I knew, though, was what Ron told me during one of our earliest teenage tripping excursions: *When you start feeling it, rub your tummy. It feels great!*

And it did! Even then—although I didn't have the
language—I realized that tummy rubbing was what
psychologists refer to as an act of *self-soothing*—much
the same as a kid sucking his thumb, or an ex-smoker
biting her nails—but whatever it was—self-soothing,
Chakra-stroking, whatever—it worked. As we tumbled
out of Beaker's van my right hand methodically
rubbed my tummy in circular motions and a giddy,
satisfying, expectant warmth made its way out of my
navel region and flowed across my chest, down my legs,
flooding out to each fingernail and toenail and tingling
my hair follicles as if an electromagnet had been
embedded in the center of my orange Navel Chakra.
I was sixteen, euphoric, in the company of friends and
surrounded by smiling, waving, friendly hippies who
were in their absolute favorite place in the entire
world: a Dead show.

Even in retrospect—*especially* in retrospect—Kingswood
was a stellar show. For some reason, soundman Dan
Healy was experimenting heavily with vocal effects that
night. This was also only days after Bob Bralove had been
hired on as the band's MIDI (Musical Instrument
Digital Interface) guru, thus allowing for a wide range
of new sounds and effects from every instrument.
Because of that, to my thinking, Kingswood '87 rates
as one of the trippiest shows of the 1980s.

The show starts straightforward enough with a decent, if undistinguished, "Touch of Grey." This was a common opener in the late 80s, and, before the song became a bona fide hit, even hardcore Deadheads really dug the tune. Given the "never say die" nature of the chorus, lyrically it would be a logical closing song: *go forward into the night, and remember, we will survive.* However, the Dead used it to great effect as an opener, an up-tempo rocking call-to-arms rallying the troops together for the night to come. Everything was going along as usual until a few verses into "Greatest Story Ever Told," when things started to get exceptionally weird. Already, Bobby's vocals were crackling with energy and Jerry's guitar carried an extra bite of distortion; there was an edge to everyone's playing, as if they were united in a musical cutting contest with the devil and all our souls were at stake. And then the Dead reached into their trippy bag of aural tricks and blew the devil ass-over-teakettle down the stairs. When Bobby hit the words "I asked him for mercy, he gave me a gun. Now and again these things just got to get done," his voice was fed through heavy reverb and started overlapping itself, the last rotation coming through clearest. At the same time, the volume on the vocals was increased, further emphasizing the delay-loop. When Brent and Jerry jumped in on the chorus, "Abraham and Isaac sitting on a fence. Get right to work if you have any sense. You know the one thing we need is a left-hand monkey wrench," the delay and vocal tweaking increased until, by the end of the chorus, their voices were smashed together, a mass of nonsensical intensity driving hard into a plea for a "left-hand monkey wrench." (It's worth noting here that novice sailors were often sent on an errand to fetch a left-handed monkey wrench; it's what's known as a "fool's errand" because there is, in fact, no such thing as a left-handed monkey wrench. This is a classic Robert Hunter prankster lyric that continues the great folkloric tradition of the fool's errand while simultaneously turning the very act of listening to the song into a fool's errand as the close listener is intellectually, if not physically, sent to find the left-handed monkey wrench in order to interpret the song. This line picks up even more resonance when partnered with the environmentalist technique of monkey-wrenching, or sabotaging, environmentally detrimental corporate workplaces [i.e., timber camps, veal farms, dam sites], a term that came into larger consciousness with the 1975 publication of Edward Abbey's environmental-themed *The Monkey Wrench Gang*.)

Based on anecdotal evidence and Dead biographies, it's likely that the band members had no intention of tweaking their vocals so heavily at Kingswood. Throughout his tenure as soundman, Dan Healy was known for "adjusting" the band's sound in ways that were more, shall we say, interactive, than the band members would've chosen.

In Phil Lesh's autobiography, *Searching for the Sound: My Life with the Grateful Dead*, he recounts,

> That was only one of the issues we'd all been having with Dan's mixing. Dan, an amateur guitar player, had special problems with Bobby. Bob's guitar would disappear from time to time, and strange electronic effects would be applied to Bob's voice or guitar. If Bob tried to say anything from the stage, Dan would drown his voice in artificial reverb so that nothing said was comprehensible. When this started happening during songs, Jerry and I decided to listen back to the recorded mixes to see what else was going on. We discovered far too many dubious mixing decisions for comfort, so we called a band meeting to discuss the problem. The band met at Mickey's ranch and listened back to some of the mix tapes, and all agreed that something had to be done. We dithered about for a while, admitting to ourselves that we were cowards who abhorred confrontation; no one wanted to be the one to tell Dan he was fired. So, wimps that we are, we had Cameron, our manager, do the deed.

Healy, of course, would argue that his experiments enhanced the music. And many Deadheads would agree. The fact is, sometimes the effects worked, and sometimes they didn't. For my money, as far as Kingswood goes, they worked just fine.

The vocal delays that started during "Greatest Story Ever Told" carried heavily into "Loser." Right from the start of the song, Jerry's voice was doubled, tripled, and powerfully accompanied by electric flourishes from Brent's Hammond B-3. "Loser" is a first set downshift in tempo, keeping the band and crowd on a manageable pace and making sure that the entire palette of musical colors gets utilized during the night. But in Kingswood, Jerry's "Loser" solo sounded like a meat grinder chewing up the right arm of a gambler who's lost everything to all the wrong people; the solo surpasses the pleading of the Loser searching for redemption and gets right to the climax where the hard-luck fucker is made to pay for his gambling excesses with bloody loss of life and limb. In fact, instead of Jerry channeling the Loser, it sounded as if he was channeling the thugs who put a hurting on the guy, teaching him a life lesson about crossing the wrong people.

As a sixteen-year-old, tripping my balls off at Kingswood, I was learning lessons that would stick. If I was tripping before the show started (which I was), the Dead hijacked that trip and took me places I never could have anticipated. First of all, I had never been to a Dead show, which means that I had never seen Deadheads lost in the reverie of the music—freak dancing. I was entranced watching them move, so lost in the music that no self-consciousness had space to survive.

It would be at least a dozen shows before I could lose myself that completely, but watching Deadheads move that night, I knew I wanted to get to that place. It was like watching a meditating person actually experience nirvana—watching the look on her face, the physical impact of bliss on the body—and suddenly understanding that nirvana was also available to you.

In a very concrete sense, I also hadn't realized that the Dead had two drummers before that night. I suppose it had just never come up in conversation, and I had never picked up on it through my albums and bootlegs. Kingswood is an amphitheater, like many others, with a shell covering the stage and seats, and a grassy hill extending past the seating area to the back of the venue. I was standing under the shell, midway back on Brent's side, and I kept rubbing my eyes to get them to focus properly. I was positive that the two drummers was a hallucination, or that there must be a mirror somewhere onstage. It was really bugging me out that I couldn't get my eyes to figure out the visual trick. But I also couldn't believe that these guys had two drummers and that I'd never realized it. Why would a band want two drummers? Considering that I already thought I was seeing double, once the band started with the echo effects on the vocals, I was a total puddle of psychedelicized teenage goo. Once they had captured both my sight and my hearing, I became convinced that the Dead

were somehow controlling everything—*everything*—that
I was experiencing: subtle changes in heat, wind, words
that people spoke, patterns in the concrete, the way a
hippie flung her hair when dancing—it all seemed to be
choreographed to enhance the show. And my trip.

I was sure that the Dead were controlling it all.

As it turns out, what I was really experiencing was a
smoking hot Dead show, pure and simple. I was also
learning something about synchronicity—the idea that,
if you are open to the possibilities, music, environment,
and personal point of view can connect in ways that
allow for new ways of perceiving the world. LSD is a
wonderful tool for lubricating the mind to accept
synchronicity. But to have any lasting impact, the individual needs to be open to the idea that synchronous
events happen constantly.

At Kingswood, I had taken synchronicity a few steps
too far. I was still having a great time, but I was also
wrestling with how a band could control so many
different factors at the same time. Meanwhile the music
was blazing and the vocals kept compressing, expanding, swirling, getting louder and then softer at seemingly
random intervals. I had stayed with Ron, Bart, and
Beaker, but it didn't matter who I was with at that
moment. We weren't talking about anything. We were
just doing our best to absorb the glorious madness.

I had collected myself a little during set break, smoked

some weed, and had a chance to pull my perspective together without the music entirely saturating my cerebral cortex. I had also finally figured out that the band did, in fact, have two drummers. In short, I was starting to get on top of my trip. Kingswood Music Theatre is inside of Canada's Wonderland Amusement Park, so half the crowd had spent the day riding roller coasters and tilt-a-whirls while tripping on acid. Between the amusement park and the far-out music, it was obvious that the band was capable of going someplace new tonight. We were all ready to pedal like hell to get that rocket ship into orbit.

The entire second set of Kingswood '87 is basically one extended jam. On their bootleg tapes (and, now, CDs), Deadheads signify the continuation of one song into the next with a right-facing arrow, meaning that the songs bleed into each other without the band ever stopping. The entire second set of Kingswood is essentially a big right-facing arrow with only one brief pause between the reprise of "Scarlet Begonias" and "Estimated Prophet": Scarlet Begonias > Fire on the Mountain > Scarlet Begonias, Estimated Prophet > Eyes of the World > Jam > Drums > Space > Spanish Jam > The Other One > China Doll > Dear Mr. Fantasy > Around and Around > Good Lovin'. Plus, the trippy effects that had punctuated the first set continued throughout the second set, linking songs together through odd sonic bridges and far-flung auditory pranks that begin before the band even kicks into "Scarlet." Before "Scarlet," there are waves of distorted sound that, for lack of a better reference point, sound like the ghostly voices that came out of the television in the movie *Poltergeist*. This was the early stages of the Dead's experiments with MIDI technology, so new sounds were about to begin popping up at every show. One of the new MIDI sounds allowed each string on Phil's bass to sound like a different disembodied voice. That's most likely where Carol Anne's haunts came from.

Blessedly, I had finally gotten on top of my trip. My smile was beaming and my body was grooving to the music. My grasp of synchronicity was coming under control, and I understood that, although the band was tearing it up, they weren't controlling the universe. Or so I thought. As "Scarlet" segued into "Fire on the Mountain," I looked around and noticed that people were turning around and facing the back of the amphitheater. Phil's bass suddenly got twice as loud and for a couple of bars it completely overtook the other instruments—fat, dense, powerful as hell. The crowd exploded with cheers. I turned around to see what everyone was looking at and was amazed to behold one of the most beautiful sunsets I had ever seen going on at the top of the grassy hill. The sun was a blaze of light hanging just on the edge of the show and illuminating hundreds of dancing Deadheads on the hill. I have seen the Dead do this numerous times over the years, matching a song to a venue or to the weather to heighten our awareness of both music and environment: playing "Looks Like Rain" on a rainy day; "Truckin'" in Buffalo; "Louie Louie" in Louisville; "Cold Rain and Snow" on a crappy, late fall East Coast day. . . . But, again, at that first concert it had never occurred to me that a band would alter their music to shape and complement their environment. I still can't think of a single band that would have the flexibility, intelligence, and chops to pull off such a thing. But at Kingswood, the Dead did it as well as I ever saw—they played "Fire on the Mountain" during that blazing sunset and, at that moment, the solar system might as well have been a backdrop arranged solely for the purpose of enhancing our collective trip. I turned my body halfway around so I could check out both the sunset and the band just by swiveling my head. I didn't want to miss either one. I wanted to take in as much as I possibly could. I was sure that such a night could never happen again. Which—in perfect Dead form—is both true and false.

The band paused briefly after "Fire" before launching into "Estimated Prophet." "Estimated" is always a high point of Bobby-singing. He loses his shit, screams, wails, and is simultaneously the prophet on the mountaintop and the misfit climbing the mountain in search of answers where none exist. In a 1977 interview with David Gans, Bobby described the genesis of "Estimated Prophet": "Essentially, the basis of it is this guy that I see at nearly every backstage door. Every time we play anywhere there's always some guy that's taken a lot of dope, and he's really bug-eyed and he's having some kind of vision. Somehow I work into his vision, or the band works into his vision, or something like that. He's got some rave that he's got to deliver. So I just decided I was gonna beat him to the punch and do it myself. I've been in that space, and I know where he's coming from."

True to form, Bobby went off on "Estimated" in Kingswood with his amazing vocal contortions dancing the fine line between brilliance and madness. This time, however, his spasms were abetted by the delay effects, so that each scream was filtered and tweaked before it reached our ears. The added twist on "Estimated" was a slowing down of the delay. As Bobby wailed out "Say no" the words got slowed down, swirled around, and spread like molasses across the music. It being 1987, as with *Poltergeist*, Nancy Reagan's ubiquitous antidrug slogan "Just Say No" was a common reference point for everyone in the amphitheater. To me, Bobby nailing the "Say no" part of "Estimated" is akin to Johnny Rotten yelling out "No future for you" on "God save the Queen." It's a direct response to governmental hypocrisy communicated by the singer with both absolute sincerity and a subtle wink to the listeners who "get it." It is not a diatribe. It is a cathartic howl.

"Estimated" segued into a bouncy "Eyes of the World" that kept everybody dancing and upbeat as day gave way to night. The energy had been flowing all day, and it was apparent that things were only going to get weirder now that darkness was upon us. The band jammed out of "Eyes" and, as Phil and Jerry fell out, Brent and Bobby laid down a funky groove before leaving the stage so that the drummers could have their way. If I still had any questions left about why a band would have two drummers, they were about to be answered. Mickey and Billy played back and forth, building up, trying out different drums, different sounds, and enjoying the complete attention of the crowd. This was no piss-break drums. We were all staying with Mickey and Billy beat-for-beat. The drummers kept the echo theme going as they worked the range of instruments in their arsenal. And then, as if to repay our rapt attention, something raucously incongruous sounded from onstage; a sound somewhere between a buzzsaw and a thunderstorm came rumbling out of the drum mix. Again, the sounds seemed to have no context in the music—they were simply a weird complement from out of the ether. Although I didn't know it at the time, it turns out that this was one of the rare occasions when the Dead miked one of the roadies Harley Davidsons and "played" it. As longtime roadie and Jerry Garcia Band road manager Steve Parish explains in his memoir *Home Before Daylight*, "I used to ride my bike right up to the stage and begin playing it with the band. See, when I was doing the drums for Mickey we built a back riser, and it became the setting for a big rhythm section, and the band wanted us to play too. So I'd jump up and started playing steel drums, maracas, whatever. We called ourselves the Rhythm Devils. Some of the guys didn't really like it all that much, but I really got into it. When the band would play "Not Fade Away," I'd fire up my bike and lay down the beat on the pipes: 'VROOM-VROOM-VROOM . . . VROOM-VROOM.'"

Whosever Harley it was, the vibrations ripped through the shell of the amphitheater, rumbling every listener from cochlea to chakra, and evoking yet more blissed-out hoots from the crowd.

After the brief "Drums," the other players came back onstage. They immediately began reprising the *Poltergeist* sounds from the second set. Again, the entire show was being linked through these strange echoes and random sounds. Often, the shift from "Space" into the first song is dramatic, like surfacing after being ten thousand micrograms under the sea. However, at Kingswood there was very little shift in intensity from "Space" into the beginning of "The Other One." Instead, "The Other

One" crept up on you—the *Poltergeist* sounds pinching
the edges of the music, and the actual notes of the song
only revealing themselves in flourishes. The band kicked
in hard for the first chorus, but then submerged back
into a hydroelectric zapped swirl. Bobby was wailing his
whammy bar with high, dissonant chords, and Phil was
dropping "Phil Bombs" on his bass all over the tune. The
vocals were hazy, reverberating, metallic with some sort
of flange effect. All over the amphitheater, you could see
the silhouette of bodies dancing in the moonlight; limbs
extending, curling, hands snaking into the sky and back
down to earth.

I was in the thick of it. My innocence had been
decimated in the first set, and by this point in the
second set, I was fully indoctrinated. I didn't know
how to dance—hell, I'd never even tried before—but my
body didn't care about that. It was going on without me.
The band downshifted into a heady "China Doll," and
the crowd swayed en masse. Jerry's voice emerged from
the craziness of the earlier music like a spiritual guide
instructing us on where we were now in the trip. Even
through the melancholy of the lyrics, "China Doll"
was comforting because it allowed Jerry to talk directly
to us. As the band played out of "China Doll," Brent
acknowledged this debt we owed to Jerry for his
guidance by shredding his vocals on "Dear Mr. Fantasy"
with a bluesy energy that paid homage to the gray

master. But Jerry wasn't content to sit back and be adored like that. He took the lead on "Dear Mr. Fantasy" and ran his fingers up and down his fretboard using speed and distortion as his primary means of communication. He even jumped in on the vocals, turning the song into more of a duet than a Brent vehicle.

The shit was thick. The night had been heavy, and the band and audience seemed equally taken with the trip—voyagers on a joint expedition. As the show headed toward a close, the band decided it was time to break out and turn this into a full-blown rock concert. They came out of "Dear Mr. Fantasy" with Bobby leading the charge on a tangy, upbeat "Around and Around." We had been bugging out on the wild sounds all night, and now it was time to purge all that intense energy. This was now a good old fashion dance party. No sooner had the band harnessed our explosive energy with "Around and Around" than they flat-out dynamited the place with "Good Lovin'." At that point, if you weren't dancing, you didn't have a pulse—or a heartbeat. With a nod to dear departed brother Pigpen, Bobby broke into a "Good Lovin'" rap while the band played calypso rhythms behind him. This night's rap was punctuated by a repeated call to "Push back, push back, push back the night!" Bobby's voice was conjuring our collective, universal need to feel and express love, and the entire crowd was lost in this rapturous expression. The second set was ending on a gloriously unified, upbeat note.

And how do you end a mind-bending show like Kingswood? You let the crowd hear something they continually, playfully clamor for: let Phil sing! The band ended the show with "Box of Rain"—a collective, feel-good tune that begs you to link arms with your neighbor and sing along at the top of your lungs.

As the crowd filtered out of Kingswood, I looked around and understood that I had just partaken in something very special. A ceremony that I had entered into almost unwittingly, but had nonetheless yearned for. Although it was only my first show, I already felt a part of the scene, one of the family among the grinning Deadheads filtering out into the parking lot. I knew I would be back again. And again.

Despite staying up all night—driving back from Canada to Rochester, and then staying up until dawn, watching the posters flutter on my bedroom walls and replaying the show in my mind—I did make it to my first day of summer school the next morning. I was still vaguely tripping from the LSD. I was absolutely flying from the pure energy of the show. I passed a hippie guy I knew from another school in the hallway, and we both exchanged a few words about the mind-altering show the previous night. More than anything, we both seemed stunned to find ourselves in this place at the end of the trip. Talk about surreal! One thing I knew for sure was that this place—summer school, an institutional hallway, surrounded by striving kids trying to succeed in the crooked game of education—was the last place I wanted to end my trip. And with the hometown show at Silver Stadium coming up the next day . . . how could I be expected to take this business of passing math so that I could, like, graduate, seriously?

I could not.

One week and two Dead shows into the summer, I dropped out of summer school. For some reason that I still don't fully understand, I was allowed to graduate in 1988 without ever completing that math course. I suppose they just wanted me out of the school. In the end, none of that mattered, though. At least in my personal history, the summer of '87 will go down as the most educational summer of my life.

CHAPTER

TWO

Morning on the Bus

Shasta has nightmares in the bus sometimes where he dreams he is falling off a cliff. It isn't uncommon for any of you to wake up unsure of where you are. You are skinny kids, and you are kids: 18, 19, 20, living on the road for the first time. The bus is a pop-up camper, and Shasta and you are compatible sleepers, so you sleep together in the top. The truth is that you know what to say to Shasta when he wakes up after a nightmare. You are used to it. Or sympathetic to it, at least. "We're in the bus, man. On tour. We're in the bus, don't worry about it, go back to sleep." Harry and whoever else is in the bus for the moment sleep below. These are small but useful rituals, and they keep things in line. The bus is your portable commune society. Shasta will be shaking, eyes wide with whatever he's brought back from the dark side of the dreams. You know what he was dreaming—it doesn't seem strange for someone who sleeps in the top bunk to dream of falling off a cliff. But there is a tenderness in this nightmare. There is vulnerability in the fact that he shares it with you and that you know what to say to him. American teenage boys aren't taught vulnerability or nurturance. They are taught aggression, competitiveness, and how to be hard. And the tenderness doesn't come naturally to you either. You have to learn it.

You wake up first and lie in the top bunk staring at the roof of the camper. Over your head is a Steal Your Face skull and lightning bolt sticker. The cold dew of morning has settled across the messy countertop and the makeshift tinted windows tattered at their plastic edges. The air is thick with the breath and the stale smoke of Deadheads who have passed out with kaleidoscopes spinning through their minds. The residue of crispy energy sunk deep into your bones has seeped out, lacing the oxygen you breathe with the spirit of your travels. You flex your toes inside your purple wool socks and sink deeper into your sleeping bag. Your head is heavy. No, your hair is heavy. Shasta spends a lot of time trying to twist his wispy, thin hair into dreadlocks. With him, it is an uphill battle that he concedes defeat to a few years later by shaving off the last

*of his aggressively receding hair and going completely
bald. But unlike Shasta, you have hair. Lots and lots of
hair. He is always trying to convince you to dread your
whole head, but you prefer to stick to sporadic dreads
laced throughout that you can untangle and re-tangle at
will. You take pride in your fluent, morphing, thriving
head of hair. You flaunt it when you dance—throwing it
back and forth, using it to cover your face, then whipping
it back dramatically at musical crescendos; it corkscrews,
it dangles, it clumps with satisfying density, it stands on
end, goes flat and straight in Denver, and puffs like a
cotton ball in Foxboro. Your beautiful, teenage Deadhead
friend Molly likes to see how many cigarettes she can hide
in your hair without any of them being visible—the record
is 26. You regularly smuggle joints, pipes, mushrooms,
acid, and whatever else needs sneaking into shows in your
hair as well. In short, your hair is your best Deadhead
feature, and you know it. Perhaps it is the one Deadhead
edge you have on Shasta. Perhaps you flaunt it too much.*

*Inside the bus, your skin is coated with the acidic
sweat of the night before; a combination of dance sweat
and the strange LSD secretions that—if bottled—you're
sure could induce secondhand psychedelic visions.*

*You all smoke cigarettes. The countertop beside the
tiny, useless sink at the foot of the bottom bunk is littered
with empty cigarette packs and used ashtrays, soda
bottles, cracker boxes, cans of ravioli, hair ties, peanut*

butter jars, half-used loaves of white bread, dirty pans,
bowls, forks, knives, spoons, beat up bootleg tapes, and the
residue of tapped-out bowls. It wasn't always that way.
Shasta was meticulous about the bus during your first
shows. At 6' 3" you have the habit of propping your feet
up on the dashboard of any car in which you ride shotgun.
But, in the early days of the bus, even that was verboten.
You remember being out on the road, away from home,
free, stoned to the gills on kind bud, laughing, smoking
cigarettes as the mild Midwestern wind whips through
your (exceptional) hair, and actually being scolded by
your friend for putting your feet on the dashboard. Hav-
ing your black Converse All Stars knocked down off the
dashboard onto the floor. Having the driver lean over
while rattling down the highway at 60 MPH (basically,
top speed for the bus) to wipe away the faint dust marks
your rubber soles have left on the vinyl. But, worst, being
on the receiving end of one of Shasta's withering looks—a
look he makes liberal use of, left eyebrow cocked, right
eyebrow lowered, right side of the mouth raised slightly
into a subtle sneer, the entire scolding pose held for a solid
10 seconds that feels much, much longer; a look that says
"you are an asshole, I know it, you know it, and I won't
tolerate it" and leaves you digging out of a psychic hole
until something, anything, breaks up the tension. That
was Shasta in the early days of the bus. But over the years
that, too, gave way to daily life. The bus is still his baby,
but it is also your home—so fuck it, you all have to live

there. A few years into it, at the end of West Coast sum-
mer tour 1990 in Eugene, Oregon, Shasta even tries to
convince you to drive the bus home—basically, he is giv-
ing it to you, at least for a while—so he can ride the St.
Stephen bus back East. The St. Stephen bus is the epitome
of hippie touring vehicles, and once you are on tour in
that, you are a full-on tour head. This was during the time
that Shasta had taken to wearing paisley patterned hippie
skirts (not as uncommon as it may sound, but certainly as
hardcore as it got in terms of dress) and was spending
more and more time with the higher echelons, the inner
circle, of the Rainbow Deadheads. He did, in fact, end up
touring in the St. Stephen bus eventually. But in 1990, in
Eugene, his plan doesn't work out and you, he, and Bart
end up driving back East together in stoned, end of tour,
communal silence.

There is no changing into sleep clothes on tour. You
sleep in what you wear every day. Your night clothes are
your day clothes and your show clothes. You always have
various necklaces strung around your neck with crystals
and rainbow-colored beads sliding back and forth across
your bare chest. Shasta has rainbow hair wraps pulling
his hair into thick clusters. You all wear multicolored,
handmade, cloth Deadhead bracelets that reek with sweat
and could—no doubt—also be wrung out to induce trips.
Your feet are dirty, but you are young and can dance for
hours without ever getting sore.

Harry snores loudly.

You are in a rest area somewhere in Michigan.

"Walk me out in morning dew, my honey. Walk me out in the morning dew today."

Harry is starting your day by singing a song. He has a horrible voice. You are all waking up, giggling in your private, family space. Harry is a funny guy. You are all in it together.

"Is it just me or was that show last night fucking smoking?" Harry pauses after the word "fucking" and hits the word "smoking" with perfect comic timing and emphasis. Living together as family, you have developed not only the vocabulary but the cadences that communicate more than the words you're speaking. He is speaking truth. He is also acknowledging the transcendent, memorable night you had spent together at the show. It is early morning, you are all waking up together, and Harry is further solidifying your family bond.

"Yeah," you sigh, locking and unlocking your knees, "it was smoking."

The flick of a lighter. Fragrant weed smoke drifts up from below.

"Nice." You hit the "N" hard and drag the "ice" out to emphasize the coolness of getting stoned first thing in the morning without having to do a damn thing to get there.

"So where are we?"

"In the bus."

A hand emerges from below holding a huge, smoking fatty. Very good pot.

"Gra-cias."

Together you drift from your private dreams into the collective dream of the bus, being on the road, remembering tunes and highlights from the night before. Harry lights up his first Marlboro of the day down below while you and Shasta hit the joint up top. You slowly pull yourselves out from the tangle of sleeping bags, fragrant pillows, and Guatemalan blankets. Shasta swings his feet down over the edge of the bunk, places one bare foot on the countertop, and eases down onto the floor of the bus, handing the joint over to Harry in the process. The front passenger seat is still turned around facing backwards from last night's post-show smoke session, so he slides into that. You make your way down and throw your legs perpendicular over Harry's legs, which are pressed against the wall of the bus. It's 8:30 A.M. Outside you hear some Deadhead yell a whooping war cry that collapses into howls that would have been more appropriate for last night's encore. Whoever it is, they haven't been to bed yet; still high—physically, mentally, psychically—from the night before.

"Those were some good doses," says Harry, dryly.

Your humor is understated, always dry, playing on the obvious to augment the absurd. You are smart, all of you, despite the fact that you all suck at school. You are smart here, in the bus, on the road, where it matters most to you.

And you are stoned.

The cocoon needs to be broken eventually. That means throwing open the sliding door to the bus and letting the outer world inside. Or more appropriately, letting your inside world out. A rest area isn't just a rest area when you're on tour. Because other Deadheads invariably end up wherever you happened to end up. It only takes minutes for the first "Hey now" to come at you when that bus door is opened. You and Harry will sit on the edge of the opening smoking cigarettes while Shasta busies himself with breakfast: peanut butter sandwiches washed down with warm orange juice. The music will already be playing nice and low inside the bus: a late 60s Pigpen "Lovelight" to get the morning started on the good foot. Your eyes are shining with weed and the triumph of having lived through a killer Dead show and good acid trip the night before.

High Times

Ask most people what drug they associate with the
1980s, and they'll probably say cocaine. Cocaine has a
slick, glossy, greasy, seamy, slutty, greedy feel that seems
to go along well with most of the popular images
beamed back from spaceship 1980s: *Less Than Zero*,
Miami Vice, Gordon Gecko, Iran-Contra, *Scarface*,
Heather Locklear, hair metal, Bret Easton Ellis, Leona
Helmsley, leveraged buyouts, "Just Say No." . . . . Most
people don't do cocaine, most people do *more* cocaine.
And that drive to get more for Me!, to hyper-accumulate
and "shop till you drop" goes along well with a drug
that violently compels one to finger-fuck every pleasure

button while bombardiering nose-first into a pile of "Peruvian marching powder." But in my suburb, at that time, cocaine was a true rarity. Every once in a while you'd hear of someone getting it, but those accounts were usually secondhand and involved either A) a cousin in another state, or B) a kid from the rival school across town. I did have one friend, Adam (a heavy partier until 11th grade when he went away to rehab and came back a preachy narc), who used to talk about doing cocaine a lot and even bought himself a little brown vial to carry it in. But I was pretty good friends with Adam, and I never actually saw any cocaine in that vial, so. . . .

As I say, cocaine was a rarity in suburbs in the 80s.

What we did have though was marijuana, acid, mushrooms, mescaline, and ecstasy. Along with beer, those were the drugs most available to us. At that time, pot was still mainly coming to upstate New York via exotic places like Mexico or California or Arizona, so it was possible to have the scene "dry up" to the point where you couldn't score a bag. In fact, there was a period in the mid-80s when the whole country seemed to dry up—no doubt due to some misguided military coup operation or drug growing eradication program targeted at impoverished third world farmers—and ever since then, small independent pot growing operations have flourished in every corner of the United States.

I suppose having supplies cut off suddenly made hundreds of stoners from Oneonta to Biloxi to Ypsilanti to Boise realize that they were smoking a plant that can grow just about anywhere they stick it in the dirt or even in the closet of their dorm room. And, before you could say *High Times*, people were growing marijuana all over the place.

Our pot came mainly through key "older brother" connections.

Our first good older brother connection was through my buddy, Jay. Jay's brother was about twenty when we were sixteen, and he was the best kind of older brother connection for the following reasons: 1) He had good pot. 2) He didn't rip us off by overcharging and/or selling us underweight bags. 3) He didn't want to meet any of the kids. Anytime an older brother wants to meet kids, you know you're in for some sort of trouble. No self-respecting older brother pot dealer cares to meet the teenage boys he's selling to. If he does, it usually means he's either sizing you up to see how bad he can rip you off, or he wants to fuck with you on a pathetic power trip—*I'm older, bigger, more experienced, AND I've got the weed!*

Jay's brother didn't want to know who we were and that was just fine with us. He'd farm out the weed to Jay in ounces or quarter pounds, and it was up to Jay to deal with his little stoner friends, collect their money ($20 for an eighth paid out in crinkled singles), and manage how to sell weed and make some money while also getting high a few times a day with his buddies. Of course, the ultimate setup was a weed-dealing older brother set up in a house where kids could actually hang out and get high. Jay had that too. His parents were divorced and, for our purposes, his dad was out of the picture. His brother stayed in his own upstairs room weighing out bags of pot and didn't care what we did as long as we didn't bother him. So that left the basement open for us to hang out and get high in. And this is where my first proper live music experiences came into play.

Jay was a drummer. The first rule of garage (or basement) bands is that practice is always at the drummer's house. This happens for the simple reason that drum kits are a pain to break down, transport, and set up: if the drummer had to do this for every band practice, that would eat up most of the practice time. Another factor is that the drummer's parents have grown accustomed to (or at least learned to tolerate) the sound of drum practice (which can never be done quietly—you can't "turn down" a drum like you can an amp, and sound-muffling drum pads get boring fast) so, to these intrepid, half-deaf parents, what's a few more instruments in the mix?

The standard move, particularly for teenage bands, is to stake out some territory in the drummer's garage or basement and turn that into the "jam room." That means that not only do the parents surrender their ears to the sound, but a sizeable part of their property to a pack of teenage kids. There is a drum kit in one corner surrounded by broken sticks, cowbells, a tambourine, brushes, and spare and destroyed drum heads. There is a huge bass amp in another corner with soda bottles lined up across the top. There is a guitar amp floating somewhere around the center, most likely propped up on a large chair or a trunk to get the sound above the mix. Depending on the band, there may be a keyboard on a cheesy aluminum stand wedged in beside the empty drum cases. There is a stained, sticky, half-broken boom box so that the garage band can listen to the famous band whose song they're butchering. And, of course, there are random patch cords, cables, microphones and mic stands, FX pedals, empty chip bags, fast food containers, music magazines, a couple of torn rock band posters on the wall, and book bags with homework papers emerging dog-eared through the broken zipper. And, for some reason, there is a stained sock poking out from under the only piece of furniture in the room: a twenty-year-old floral print couch, stained by years of juice, pizza, and syrup. This is the couch that the drummer grew up with and on which he occasionally had potty-training accidents; the couch he cuddled on while reading with his parents or

watching television with his family; the couch he stayed
on all day while home sick from school. . . . And now
that couch is too broken-down for his parents, an
embarrassment. But it suits the jam room just fine. So
the drummer drags it out to the garage or down to the
basement, and there it stays, proof that this jam room is
practically like the band's own studio apartment.

Now take a closer look at that stained sock under the
couch. The toe is just visible under the tattered fringe
covering the couch legs. Pick it up and study it. What
are those brown marks? They almost look like lipstick
stains, the same shape as two heavily painted lips on a
cheek or mirror. But the stain is dark brown and
repeated all over the sock from toe to top. Look even
closer: what is it stained with?

Reach a little farther underneath the couch and
you'll find your first clue: a small bong, a bowl, a one-
hitter, a steamroller fashioned from a paper towel roll,
tape, and aluminum foil, a soda can crushed in at one
end and strategically punctured by an awl with tiny
little holes on top and a larger hole around the side.
Perhaps there's even a tray under there to break up
weed on, a tray covered with loose grains and a few
dozen seeds that the kids talk about planting, but never
will. Perhaps there is a pack of Zig Zag rolling papers, a
greasy roach clip, a pile of stems, some chewed to a
stringy pulp on one end.

Yes, the only thing better than a good teenage jam room is a teenage jam room you can get high in. And, because most suburban parents, even the drummer's parents, don't approve of marijuana smoking, teenage kids learn ways to disguise the telltale signs of pot use. Once the jam room is set up, the battle is half-won: no parents want to walk around in a space that teenage kids spend that much time hanging out in and once the room is set up, it's seldom taken apart. So, right off the bat, the physical space is semiprivate. If, like Jay, your parents are divorced and your primary parent works long hours, then you've got another factor working in your favor.

But you don't want to get too blatant about the situation. You don't want to risk blowing it all and losing your space. So you keep an old sock or a towel hidden in the room and you exhale your hits into that. It's surely not as satisfactory as unloading a lungful of pot smoke into a stream of sunshine, but it is more discreet. Voila, the smoke is absorbed into the sock, leaving only black lip marks as remnants. Then the sock is tucked under the couch along with the rest of the pot smoking paraphernalia. Once you get to college, you learn about stuffing dryer sheets into paper towel rolls and blowing your hits through the contraption—an excellent way to smoke pot in a dorm room undetected. There is smoke, yes, but it comes out smelling "Spring

Fresh." The downside is that your room smells like extremely cheap perfume all the time—which is still better than getting busted by an overzealous RA. But while the dryer roll is a great dorm tool, the overpowering, sickly sweet, and lingering smell and the fact that actual smoke comes out makes it less perfect for a teenage jam room. So, for teenagers, it's best to stick with the sock.

Jay had everything going for him. He was the drummer. He had a jam room in his basement. His parents were divorced and his mother worked. His brother sold weed out of his bedroom and didn't want to know us kids. Plus, he lived in the Village of Pittsford, which meant we could all walk there from school. Many kids could walk home from Jay's too. This potent brew made for my first pot smoking live music encounters.

And Jay wasn't stupid about it either. He was a cool, good-looking, popular guy, and he didn't feel the need to pack his basement with kids just to make friends. So the scene in Jay's basement was exclusive—close pot smoking, music loving friends only—and made for a familial vibe. I spent many hours sprawled out on the couch in Jay's basement, stoned to the gills on his brother's weed, listening to Jay's primary high school band, The Scene, work out sloppy garage band versions of songs by Pink Floyd, The Doors, Led Zeppelin, and even a few more modern tunes by U2 and R.E.M. As the youngest of four kids, I had always been surrounded by rock music of one kind or another. But those afternoons in Jay's basement were the first times I really thought about what went into those songs: the working parts, the musicians, the bass part, the guitar solo, the drum beat. Listening to the band stop and start, honing the various passages of a song, screwing up and having to restart and so forth, made me appreciate both the effort of making rock-n-roll and the basics of band dynamics. Human dynamics too. I was there, stoned on the couch and checking it all out, but I was also absorbing the whole scene. I was thinking about every little part, getting an education in both music and people.

CHAPTER FOUR

Oakland Coliseum, December 28, 1987

Set 1: *Feel Like a Stranger > Franklin's Tower,
New Minglewood Blues, Row Jimmy, Far
from Me, When I Paint My Masterpiece >
Sugaree, Hell in a Bucket*

Set 2: *China Cat Sunflower > I Know You Rider,
Cumberland Blues, Man Smart/Woman
Smarter > Drums > Space > The Wheel >
Truckin' > Smokestack Lightnin' > Black
Peter > Sugar Magnolia*

Encore: *Black Muddy River*

You're seventeen years old. Your entire family has come to California for a family vacation. You will go to the Rose Bowl parade and the football game. You will go to the coast at Carmel and stare at the sea lions. You will go to Disneyland. Even though there are six people in your family, you have been allowed to take one friend—Ron—on this trip because you are generally surly when it comes to family trips, and besides, Ron's family used to take you to Martha's Vineyard with them. This is your parents' chance to reciprocate to Ron's parents.

But you and Ron have your eyes on one thing only: the first two shows of the 1987 New Year's run at the Oakland Coliseum. You mail-ordered tickets before you left town. The tickets are colorful and covered with glitter. If this were Charlie and the Chocolate Factory, *these would be your golden tickets. They are the most important piece of luggage you brought with you to California.*

Your family is staying in a hotel in Oakland. Who knows what they'll be doing while you are at the show: going to dinner, sightseeing, looking at the ocean . . . whatever. Your father takes you and Ron to the BART station where you will take a train to the coliseum. This is the first time in California for both you and Ron. You've been to a handful of shows between you, but you are still both new to the scene. You are wearing your tie-dyes, jeans, and sneakers. Your hair is shaggy and your face is broken out with zits. You are giddy for the show and hungry for West Coast drugs.

*The subway is filled with Heads making their way
to the show. Even riding to the venue, you notice differ-
ences between the West Coast and the East Coast scenes.
The West Coast crowd is mellower, more laid-back. You
realize that they simply get more Grateful Dead than you
get in the East. More opportunities to see the band and to
catch Jerry Band shows and affiliated gigs in between
tours. So there's not the hard jones of waiting for the band
to come your way. That hard crackle of energy isn't there.
The vibe is more chilled out and the people seem lighter,
not as intense.*

   *You get to the parking lot, and the scene is swinging. In
short order, you and Ron score some beautiful-looking bud
that's identified to you as Alaskan Indica. The bag is heavy,
and the bud is light green and covered with white hairs
and tiny crystals. It looks like it could glow in the dark. It
could power a space station. It could send out waves that
could stone an entire United Nations meeting if only they
were smart enough to try it.*

   *You are thrilled. You score acid. You smoke the Indica.
You eat some mushrooms. You eat the acid. You smoke
more Indica. You eat your first "space cake," which is
basically a kind bud muffin-cookie hybrid. The space cake
tastes like someone sprinkled sugar on a dandelion, so
you know it'll get to work fast and hard.*

   *Everything starts kicking in. You and Ron are wander-
ing the parking lot whacked out and breathless on drugs.
It is only California, but it might as well be Pluto. You feel*

like astronauts or explorers stumbling on an Aztec civilization. You are the first of your crew to hit a West Coast show. And, although it isn't an actual New Year's show—epic among Dead rituals—it's a show on the New Year's run. You and Ron are rubbing your tummies as you've learned to do to soothe the buzz. You are walking around the parking lot taking in the world through enormous full-moon pupils.

You are already waiting in line when the doors open to get into the show. You went to last night's show and have more of an idea this time on how to proceed. You and Ron hustle your way through the concrete hallways and blaze through the entryway where the empty room opens before you: it is a Roman coliseum, and you are simultaneously lions and gladiators. Already, Deadheads are streaming down the aisles to get the best floor space. You and Ron hustle your way down the stairs and make for the floor. The taper section is bristling with microphone stands three-quarters back next to the soundboard, and serious-looking hippies are checking and rechecking their decks and gear through their own dilated pupils. For them, this is both work and play. For you: strictly play.

Deadheads have spread out Mexican blankets to mark their space. People are batting beach balls across the floor. The coliseum already reeks of kind bud smoke, patchouli, body odor, and the singular tangy smell of acid sweat. Or maybe that's just you. A woman with a loose peasant dress and long dreadlocks stands up and crows like a rooster as loud as she can. She stands back and listens proudly as it echoes and reverberates around the scene. She's answered back by a trilling call reminiscent of Persian warriors charging headlong into battle. Soon the air is cluttered with catcalls, rooster crows, and assorted bellows pushing the energy level in the room higher and higher. People are sitting cross-legged in circles facing each other in conversation. It seems all drug laws have been suspended in the coliseum. People are passing pipes and ingesting LSD and space cakes as if it's the most natural thing in the world to take drugs in public. No hiding, no shame. Some wasted version of heaven.

You and Ron are among the youngest people there. That is obvious. The room is filled with older, rode hard hippies and crunchy, organic long-hairs who look remarkably tanned, limber, and healthy. There's no doubt about it: you are tripping your balls off. Every once in a while you and Ron look at each other and just start laughing.

You're here. You made it. The Dead at the Oakland Coliseum.

You've settled on the floor thirty yards from the stage. Brent's side, of course. You smoke some more of the Alaskan Indica, passing it over to your neighbors and receiving back different pipes in return. There are some giddy non sequiturs, but you don't say much while you're waiting for the show to start because you're tripping too hard for conversation. Plus, what is there to say? The situation is post-verbal.

The coliseum is filled and the energy is peaked out. It seems like everyone around you is tripping—and they are. The entire room is dosed, high, and ready to move. The lights go down and the room explodes into applause and catcalls: the show is about to start. Everyone who had been seated on the floor passing pipes now springs to his or her feet and starts swaying and jumping up and down in preparation for the dancing to come. You make your way to your feet too, but not as steadily as those around you. You've had too much too fast. The room is tilted to the right like a funhouse. You are standing in the middle of a quasar. The sounds are fucked. Everything is fucked. The spotlights onstage come up—the band has materialized there as if their molecules were willed into being by your sheer collective desire to see them. This is too much. The Dead kick into "Feel Like a Stranger" to open the show, and you pass out. You're down. Unconscious. Flat on your back in the middle of the coliseum while the band tears the walls off reality and blasts the roof apart so we can all see the stars.

You regain consciousness. A group of Deadheads is standing in a circle looking down at you. Ron is standing among them with a goofy grin on his face. After all, this can't be real. Can it? Does it matter? A security guard is standing over you. You expect him to hustle you off the floor, but he doesn't. He's actually cool about it. He's seen this before. He's West Coast all the way, and he knows he's at a Dead show. Plus the Heads are there to help you out and reassure the guard that you're fine. You're just young, overexcited, took a little too much. Let him dance, they say, and he'll be fine.

Deadheads and the security guard help you to your feet. Ron is still standing back, still not sure of what's happening. But he's starting to get the idea. The band is scorching "Feel Like a Stranger" like it's their God-given right to paint a sonic picture of your twisted psyche for everyone to hear. It is perfect. The tune couldn't be more fitting. Because you are a stranger. You are seventeen years old, tripping your face off three thousand miles away from home, and you've only recently regained consciousness. But the consciousness you've regained is not the same one you left behind. People are patting you on the back. Encouraging you to dance it off. Someone hugs you. Ron slaps your back in a brotherly, "shake-it-off" way, and points at the stage as if to say, "Remember. Look. We're here. There they are! The Dead!"

And you do. You don't fight it. Your father will pick you up at the BART station after the show and drive you and Ron back to the hotel. You will still be tripping hard. You will take the longest elevator ride of your life back up to your hotel room with you, Ron, and your dad standing there in silence, watching the floors flash by in neon red numbers. You will go to the Rose Bowl parade and the football game later that week. You will go to the coast at Carmel, stare at the sea lions and take pictures with your family sitting on the rocks. You will go to Disneyland. But first there is the Dead show. This show. You are here now. You do feel like a stranger, and this is your song to welcome you to the scene. Bobby says it all: "You know it's gonna get stranger. Some things we just know."

The Town
and
the Village

Our town was broken into five public elementary schools (Allen Creek, Thornell Road, Park Road, Barker Road, and Jefferson Road) that fed into two public high schools (Mendon and Sutherland). As it broke out, the kids from Thornell Road and Park Road ended up attending Mendon High School, while the kids from Allen Creek and Jefferson Road went to Sutherland. The Barker Road kids got split down the middle—some to Sutherland, some to Mendon—based on property lines. Once upon a time, Pittsford Mendon and Pittsford Sutherland were rival schools. Mendon was considered a little more highbrow—more Mendon than Pittsford,

if you catch my meaning. The school was newer, in
much better condition, and the way we saw it the girls
were all blond (we wanted to sleep with them) and the
boys were a little bit too cocky (we wanted to be like
them). Of course, at this writing, the two schools have
merged most of their athletic programs and Sutherland
has undergone massive renovations, thus dissolving the
thrust of the rivalry. But at one time that rivalry meant
something, and the two schools barely mixed. In any
event, the five elementary schools dumped into two
junior highs. The Park Road, Thornell, and some Barker
Road Elementary students went to Barker Road Junior
High. The Jefferson Road, Allen Creek, and the rest of
the Barker Road students went to Mendon Center
Junior High.

Thus, in 1982, I broke out of my Allen Creek Elementary School bubble into the wild world of Mendon
Center Junior High.

Despite the fact that we were all dumped into junior
high together, the two camps that had formed at Allen
Creek and Jefferson Road remained amazingly cohesive
throughout junior high and high school at Sutherland
(the Barker Road kids were basically divvied up and
folded into one of the two groups). We were all
friends—especially the partiers among us—but we
never forgot which elementary schools we'd started
out in. Those lines were actually much clearer than
one might imagine.

The Allen Creek kids (and I was one of them) were nicer. I realize that sounds self-serving, but bear with me. By "nicer" I mean that we tended to come from outwardly stable families, meaning that our parents were white–collar middle-management or higher, a higher percentage of them were still married, they had more education, and social graces had been drilled into their kids (us) while growing up. We knew our Ps & Qs, so to speak, and could turn them on when we needed to make a good impression. Allen Creek students were culled mainly from the suburbs, not the Village of Pittsford, so our homes were a little bit nicer, newer, and our parents had more disposable income.

We looked nice. We spoke nice.

That was us: nice white suburban kids.

The Jefferson Road kids were mainly from the Village of Pittsford. The Village of Pittsford is absolutely quaint—it always has been. It's the oldest village in Monroe County and includes the county's first school (1794), the first library (1803), the first permanent church (1807), the first post office (1811), and the first newspaper (1815). The first house in town was built by Israel Stone in 1789, and in 1813 the town was named Pittsford in honor of the Vermont birthplace of Colonel Caleb Hopkins, a farmer and hero of the War of 1812. Pittsford is proud of its heritage. The town has a reputation for being the ritzy suburb of Rochester, and particularly in the late 1990s, they made a real effort to live up to that reputation by adding more upscale stores and giving the village four corners a major facelift.

But when I was in junior high and high school, the town was a little shabbier. Perfectly shabby. The village houses were less expensive than the antiseptic sprawling suburban homes, so parents could get their kids into Pittsford schools and still work blue-collar jobs. And this was where many of the Jefferson Road kids were raised. More of their parents were divorced; more of them smoked, drank, swore; and they were less likely to give you the big phony suburban welcome when you came shambling in the door to see their kids. More likely it would be, "Wipe your feet. He's upstairs." And then back to whatever they'd been doing, hardly looking up to see who'd just come in.

Obviously, this lifestyle fascinated us kids from Allen Creek. The freedom, the decadence, the anonymity of coming and going without dictatorial parental scrutiny. It all felt very real.

Easily the best example of the village esthetic was the home of Tony and Jimmy Silvio.

Twins. Hellions. And, not coincidentally, they provided our other good older brother pot connection.

On the surface, Tony and Jimmy's situation was not much different than Jay's: their parents were divorced, their mother worked long hours as a waitress at a prime rib restaurant, they lived in the village, and their older brother occasionally sold them pot. But Tony and Jimmy were, in a deeper sense, very different from Jay. Despite the divorce, Jay's mother—and his father, albeit from a distance—were both affectionate, supportive, nurturing, and the family was close-knit. But as long as I had known Tony and Jimmy they had been left on their own. Not only did their mother work long hours, but when she was home she was not particularly involved with the boys. Don't get me wrong, it's not that she didn't love them. But Tony and Jimmy were the last of seven children, and their father was a cantankerous bastard who'd cut out after she got pregnant with the twins. He had started a new family shortly after leaving Mrs. Silvio. This pushed him farther out of the picture and left her to raise these last two entirely on her own.

Like Jay's brother, Jimmy and Tony's older brother, Mark, didn't want much contact with us kids. But, most likely due to the broken family situation, he also didn't have any qualms about ripping us off whenever he felt like it. He'd seen us enough to know that we were punk kids who would snatch up whatever drugs we could get our hands on, and had no problem charging us top dollar for low-quality product. Of course, this rip-off usually came down to us through Jimmy and Tony— Mark ripped them off, so they had to stiff us—but we never held it against the twins. For that matter, we never really held it against Mark either (not that he would've cared). Mark's overpriced shitty Mexican ditchweed got us through the horrible marijuana drought of the 80s. And for that we'd always be grateful.

Jay's house had provided fun, a brotherhood of sorts, and helped me gain a deeper appreciation of music. But, to be blunt, Jimmy and Tony's house had almost none of those redeeming qualities. Their house was about partying, plain and simple. There was a sort of brotherhood, yes, but nobody really watched each other's backs there. Rip-offs were common. Guys fooled around with each other's girlfriends. Shit was talked. Slap-boxing turned into fistfights. Where Jay's house was essentially a cool band practice space, the Silvios' was more like a combination clubhouse and halfway house for wayward teens. If you got kicked out of your house or just had a major blowout with your folks and had nowhere to go—you went to the Silvios'. At bare minimum, the twins would be there to hang out with. But chances are there would be at least one or two other kids there as well. Not just kids either, but bad kids. Village kids. Kids who liked to smoke and drink. Kids who hooked up with girls and then talked about it to all their buddies (around the Silvios' kitchen table). Kids who did poorly at school. The Silvios had a beat-up pool table and dog-eared deck of cards. You could smoke anywhere in the house. If necessary, you could sleep on their couch.

The furniture, the house itself, was beat up in a way that facilitated partying.

In many ways, Tony and Jimmy Silvio were the quintessential Jefferson Road village kids.

Of course, we Allen Creek kids who were interested in partying were solidly impressed by the Jefferson Road kids as soon as we met them at Mendon Center Junior High. Up to that point, the extremes of our experimentation had been smoking dried maple leaves rolled up in brown paper lunch bags and downing shots of vinegar as if it was whiskey. Yet, even as the two groups formed a loose cadre of partiers moving into Sutherland High School, we never lost track of those elementary school ties. The Allen Creek kids were always the Allen Creek kids: our allegiances stayed mainly with each other. The same went for the Jefferson Road kids. And the Barker Road kids, well, they just had to sort things out for themselves.

Aside from Jay's and the Silvios', the major hangout destinations where most of our partying and socializing took place outside of school were outdoors. At least two of them were nestled beside the Erie Canal, which runs through the middle of Pittsford. The local section of the Erie Canal opened in 1822; roughly five years later Pittsford was incorporated as a village. Between canal construction and trading, the town prospered. Nearly two hundred years later, the canal is only a tourist attraction. But, for kids who grew up in Pittsford, the Canal Park and The Trestle are legendary spots.

In 1997 a fourteen-year-old girl named Shelby and a sixteen-year-old boy named Jackson were hit by a train and killed on the trestle in Pittsford. Anyone who had hung out on the trestle could tell you that this would happen eventually. The accident was ten years after I graduated from high school, ten years after my group partied on and ruled the trestle. But in some ways, even though I had never met those two kids, it still felt like the end of an era. The trestle was, at once, innocent and decadent. It was a Never-Never Land of teenage sex, substance abuse, and stupid hormonal bravado. But the decadence was still experimental. All of our clumsy attempts to unlatch bras and guzzle stolen liquor were done at the hemline of the town's housecoat, literally within the shadow of the town center, making us more rebels in the Eddie Haskell tradition than the Jim Stark line. We were not yet good at being bad.

The trestle extends over the Erie Canal parallel to East Avenue where it intersects Monroe Avenue to create the four corners of Pittsford (at which point the roads turn into Main and State Street, respectively). In the early days of the Erie Canal, including its construction, beasts of burden were used to haul barges along the waterway. As a result, well-maintained paths run beside the canal to this day. These paths, now used by joggers and bikers instead of oxen, are collectively referred to as canal trails. To Pittsford kids in the 70s and 80s the canal trails represented early freedom, isolated highways that linked parts of Pittsford together via routes so sheltered from car traffic that even the most overprotective parent would be hard pressed to argue against a kid using them. I was fortunate enough to have access to a canal trail only two-thirds of a mile away from my house—my portal from the suburbs to the village. So, starting from age twelve, I used the canal trails to escape home, to find new places to explore and new trouble to get into away from the cul-de-sac where I'd grown up.

The trestle is an enormous old iron behemoth. It is black and strewn with graffiti. Decades of broken beer bottles have left shiny bits of green and brown glass nestled between rocks leading up to the trestle and on every flat surface not rattled by speeding trains. Large rocks around the structure are sloppily spray-painted gold and blue—Pittsford Sutherland's school colors— and repainted regularly to update the year in which the *Seniors Rule!* The trestle is only accessible via the canal trail. No one's parents could suddenly shine their car headlights onto the trestle and bust you in an act of mid-deviance. If you wanted to get to the trestle, you rode a bike or walked. Once you arrived, you stashed your bike in the woods where a short dirt and debris-cluttered path winds around the concrete pillar that forms the eastern base of the trestle and dumps you off immediately at the railroad tracks.

Most people are disgusted when I tell them about "scum jumping." And they're right to be. Scum jumping is disgusting. Scum jumping was the term we used for— quite simply—jumping off the train trestle into the Erie Canal. For anyone who hasn't seen the Erie Canal, the water can best be described as looking like chocolate milk. It is dirty, brown, smelly water. Not toxic, that I'm aware of, but certainly very, very dirty. Growing up, there was wonderful folklore about kids scum jumping and plummeting through rotting cow carcasses floating down the canal. This never actually happened, mind you, but it was still gospel to kids in Pittsford. And, as with all legends—be they urban or suburban—the story, though bogus, was meant to convey real danger. There *was* debris floating in the canal. Mostly fallen limbs from the trees bordering the canal trail. There were also sub-merged pillars and supports. There were rats. There were dead carp as big as watermelons. In short, there were all sorts of things floating in the canal that you didn't want to jump off a bridge and land on. But still, we jumped.

Interestingly enough, although we also hung out regularly in the canal park in the Village of Pittsford (behind the town courthouse), we never would've considered wading into the canal there. *That* would've been disgusting. We weren't merely swimming. We were jumping.

Scum jumping.

The trestle was the unofficial meeting ground for the suburban kids and the village kids. It was accessible to us all, and no one was up there to be *good kids*. It was illegal to hang out on the trestle in the first place, so merely showing up there meant you had taken a step toward lawlessness. You were ready to go down that path. Every boy I hung out with in high school scum jumped. Every one of us had trestle and scum-jumping stories to tell. My most memorable scum-jumping story was much like that of the two kids who were killed there in 1997.

Every once in a while, kids played chicken with trains; they would wait on the edge of the tracks as the train approached. Chicken was best played with at least two kids so you could gauge how brave you were based on whether you were the first kid to jump. It was also best played to an audience so that tales of your derring-do could spread like war stories through the halls at school or later on while smoking a bowl at the canal park. I was not a kid who played chicken. I didn't climb to the highest parts of the trestle. I was never one of the kids we admiringly called *crazy*. But still, the stereotypical parental question, "If all of your friends jumped off a bridge, would you?" was answered by me with a definitive "Yes." I was a regular at the trestle. And one day, though I didn't intend to, I played my own game of chicken with a train.

Teenage drug culture has many rules and signposts. The signposts are primarily visual and have to do with staking out territory in your own personal drug niche. In the late 1980s the rules governing the signposts were pretty simple. You could tell who the stoners were based on how they dressed. If you wore a T-shirt with a metal band on it (the coolest at that time being Metallica), usually with a flannel shirt draped over it (even in the summer), with jeans and hi-top sneakers with the laces untied—you were a metalhead stoner. If you wore a plain tie-dye, or a tie-dye featuring any 1960s band (e.g., Pink Floyd, The Doors, Led Zeppelin, The Jimi Hendrix Experience), with a flannel draped over it (even in the summer), and a beat up jeans jacket with a pack of Marlboros tucked into the breast pocket—you were a hippie stoner. The Deadhead stoners were an exclusive subset of hippie stoner and largely eschewed tie-dyes for primary colored Grateful Dead T-shirts that were subtler and less common. Deadhead stoners also often had the back of their jeans jackets painted to illustrate their Dead affiliation, thus negating any subtleties gained by not wearing tie-dye. There were a few pockets of goth stoners (pre-Columbine trench coats being the main indicator there), but not enough to create a real subset. There were also the casual, week-end pot smokers scattered throughout the preppy set (a term that actually signified an identifiable point of view and socioeconomic striving in the 80s), the serious students, the hardcore jocks (as opposed to the stoner jocks, of which there were many), and the dorks. But, mainly, if you were a full-fledged part of high school drug culture at that time, you either identified with the hippies or the metalheads.

Within these two groups—hippies and metalheads—there were, of course, hierarchies that would be invisible to outsiders. For instance, an Iron Maiden shirt signified a more sophisticated perspective than a Metallica shirt. Metallica may have been more contemporary—and better, some would argue—but only the hardcore metal heads would wear an Iron Maiden shirt to school in the 1980s. For the hippies, one example of a signpost designating hierarchy might be footwear. Did you wear a Pink Floyd tie-dye with Docksiders? If so, you were probably a hippie stoner who hadn't fully committed to the hippie stoner lifestyle (still holding on to preppy aspirations), thus lower on the food chain than, say, someone wearing the same tie-dye with beat up Converse All Stars. Definitely lower than, say, someone wearing knee-length brown buckskin boots with dangly leather fringe at the top (guilty).

But being included in a drug culture group wasn't enough. Once inside, it was important to differentiate yourself. You had to stand out. Were you an expert on The Doors? Or on Floyd? Could you get high-quality bootlegs? Did you show up to school high every day, or wait until lunch? Did you always have weed? Or always latch onto people who had weed? Each person had his or her own niche, and it was important not to step too far into someone else's space lest you risk being ostracized and branded a poseur.

Another way to stand out was through the paraphernalia that you used. If you seldom had your own weed, but always had a good pipe on you—you were good to go. As we got older and started driving, the bowls and rolling papers of our youth morphed into bongs that we could hide under our seats or in the trunk. That's when things got really creative.

My crew of Allen Creek hippie stoners (again, although we were completely merged with the Jefferson Road stoners by then, both groups always remained most loyal to their original groupings) used to regularly chip in on bongs that we would then name and share. Some bong names that I remember are: Cherry Forever, Yaweh, Baby Blue, and The Big Ole. But the king of all bongs—the six-foot-tall Graffix bong owned by the Silvio brothers—was named Herman Munster. (I would be remiss not to mention the king metalhead bong here as well. Because metalheads were also closely identified with the gearheads from shop and auto-tech class, their best bong was built into the dashboard of a major metalhead's car. You pulled the tube out just below the tape deck and the bowl was disguised in a dashboard vent. The water was poured down the vent as well. Frankly, I'm still not sure how the thing actually worked.) Because we shared bongs, it was common for us to choose meeting spots where a few guys could get together (at lunch, after school, during free periods, etc.) and collectively smoke. One of those places was, of course, the trestle.

There are a handful of instances that stand out in my mind as signposts to the possibility of an early death. Two of them involve the Erie Canal. In one of the scenarios I am eleven years old walking with my friend Sean over the canal in February. Every year the canal is drained for the winter and allowed to refill in the spring. But there is always some water that never drains and can be surprisingly deep in spots. In this case, Sean and I were walking over the ice alongside Schoen Place—a quaint row of shops, restaurants, and bench areas—just before the Main Street bridge in the Village of Pittsford. That's where I fell through the ice. In retrospect, Sean says that I walked straight into a big hole in the ice. As much as I cringe at that explanation—

he's probably right. I was most likely waving my hands, laughing, talking about something, and not paying attention to where I was going when—plop—I was falling into the dirty, freezing cold water.

As I said, this was a "signpost to the possibility of an early death." The truth is that the water wasn't deep enough for me to completely submerge in. But I will always remember—in a way that surpasses my brain and goes straight to my chest—the feeling of dropping away. The flash realization that the thing you were always taught to watch out for while skating or playing outside in the winter was, in fact, upon you. I remember falling and wondering when I would stop. The water passed my knees, my waist, and by the time I had sunk to mid-chest it was apparent that things were getting serious. Fortunately, I hit the mucky bottom with my snowmobile boots and pushed off enough to lift myself over the thin edge of the ice surrounding the hole. The ice cracked, and I fell back into the water twice before I made it out (of course, hypothermia is as real as drowning, but to me the possibility of freezing doesn't carry that same gut-fear induced by breaking through the ice), but eventually I flopped out like a soaking, chunky little seal bundled in layers of wet winter clothes. I was shaking, still unsure the ice would support my weight. Sean—still the best outdoorsman I have ever known—wisely hustled us off the ice. The walk back to Sean's home outside the Village was miserable, I was covered with mud, freezing, stinking of canal water, and humiliated by the whole incident.

Still, falling through the ice ranks second to getting my foot caught between railroad ties on the trestle while a train closed in on me. A group of us, I don't remember who, were partying on the trestle. Getting high. Maybe drinking, maybe not. We spotted the familiar sight of a train coming down the tracks. Usually, the train blew its whistle, we all stepped off the tracks on the closest edge of the trestle, the train went past, we whooped and yelled, maybe threw rocks or a bottle at it, and then went back to partying on the tracks once the train was gone. For some (stoned) reason, though, this one time I decided to walk all the way across the bridge before the train came. This wasn't an act of courage or bravery. Again, I was most likely caught up in my own thoughts and not paying enough attention to the real— in this case, very real—world. I had a good lead on the train, so while ill-advised, the situation wasn't imminently dangerous. The trestle is about 50 yards long and I had made it three-quarters of the way across the tracks before my foot got caught. I don't remember the moment that my foot slid between the thick, blocky wooden ties. What I do remember is trying to pull back my foot and my foot not budging. I tried again. No movement. I was still a good 10 yards from the end of the trestle where I could safely get off the tracks. The train blew its whistle. I tried again—nothing. I reached down to my knee to get a better lift while yanking my foot up and forward toward the end of the trestle. My foot moved a little, but mostly my shin just jammed hard against the wooden tie. Pain shot from my shin up my leg, adding to the panic welling inside of me. The pain was real. My foot being stuck was real. The train about to pass onto the trestle and the whistle sound filling my skull were very real. This was my first death. I was holding my leg, stuck on a bridge, a stoned teenager in hippie clothes waiting for a train to end my life. But I didn't die. At last, my foot came out of the tracks, allowing me to scurry across the remaining ties and leap off the edge of the trestle before the train passed. I can still picture the look on my friends' faces as we all realized what had just occurred. I can feel the huge, painful swelling on my shin from my attempts to pull my foot free. But all that matters now is that I didn't die. I only tasted death.

Ten years later, Pittsford teenagers Shelby and Jackson were not so fortunate. I did not know them, nor do I know the details surrounding their death aside from the basic facts. She got stuck, he went back to help her—neither one of them made it out in time. Still, every time I pass the trestle, I think about those two kids. Based on the graffiti around the trestle and the bouquets of flowers that still appear there regularly, Shelby and Jackson are still very present in the thoughts of their friends and family as well. I lost three friends in my teens: two by suicide, one by a car crash. Somehow the deaths of teenagers always seem the most senseless; we are vulnerable as small children and increasingly vulnerable as we move into old age, but teenagers are so strong, cocky, resilient. They appear farthest from death than at any other time of life.

Show Time

Anxiety hits a peak when you're just starting to get off on good blotter acid and it's time to go into the show. You gather in the bus. It's time to pull some things to- gether: ticket, weed, best dancing gear, ticket, another dose, ticket, cigarettes, ticket, lighter, ticket, friends, ticket, ticket . . . . Do I have my ticket? It's okay: you've got your ticket. Take one last look at it and then put it back in your red Guatemalan fanny pack. Don't look at it again. It's starting to get soggy from the perspiration on your hands; perspiration that breaks out every time you worry that you don't have your ticket, thus forcing you to check your ticket and get the ticket even soggier. Whatever you do, don't rip the stub. If you rip the stub, the ticket is worthless—they won't let you in. Even if you have both pieces, they won't let you in. They'll think you're lying. That you stole the ticket. Everyone will go inside and you'll be stuck outside the show in the parking lot, no music, tripping by yourself, locked out of the bus 'cause everyone is inside and you don't have a key.

Is that a tear in the perforation?

You look around and see your tour brother tripping and trying to pull it together too. Harry keeps fumbling through his fanny pack, then sighing deeply, smiling at you with huge dilated pupils that, at once, communicate— help me, this is the best, heaven is here, hell is too close, the show is about to start, help me, love, love, help— before they swivel back into the fanny pack looking for the one indefinable object that will signal "all ready" once it is found. It never will be. Getting on top of your trip ain't that easy. But shuffling through those options is part of the fun. Bart is sitting in the passenger seat of the bus with the visor mirror pulled down in front of him. He's wearing tight cutoff jeans, rope sandals, and a faded skull-and-roses tank top that looks like he'd worn it every day since 1976. He keeps pulling his hair back into a pony-tail. Tight. Very tight. He smoothes it down (he is in a bald race with Shasta, thus obsessed with his hair during trips) and pulls it back with a purple scrunchy. Then he checks it in the rear-view mirror. He looks at the scraggly

growth of beard on his cheeks. Picks at a zit on his chin.
Then whips the scrunchy out of his hair with a dramatic
flourish and shakes the ponytail out until his hair is flying
in long, loose, dry tufts around his eyes. He smiles a little
at this in the mirror. Then frowns. Checks the zit.

In this group, Bart and Shasta are the most serious.

Sissy is leaned up against the outside of the bus laugh-
ing for no particular reason. From what you can tell,
someone just walked past and said something strange,
foreign, and hilarious about some people a few cars
down—some local douche bags sucking nitrous like
mother's milk. Sissy is wearing cutoff army pants and
Tevas that are always coated in a fine layer of dust. He is
also in early stage male-pattern baldness and also has
long hair and a beard. You consider probing for a deeper
understanding of the humor, but then you realize that
Buddha is standing with Sissy and laughing too. Since
there are two of them, it's possible that their laughter
could turn on you if you invade the giggle-space. You
don't want that worm turning—especially before going
into the show.

Friends stop by on their way into the show. Some get
you high (as if you could get higher, but still . . . you take
the hits out of preglass state-of-the-art antler bowls).
Some are tripping harder than you. They try to converse,
but no one can make it happen—the smart ones split that
scene fast with a little jig, a kind smile, maybe a parting

hug and "have a good show." The more severely lost souls linger on the edges of the group, trying to make eye contact (why bother?) and then looking away—occasionally trying to start conversations that don't make any sense to them or you or anyone who might be eavesdropping. You know better, though. You know that conversation during an acid trip is pointless until the very tail end of the trip, when you're coming down, maybe a few paisley patterns still pulsing in your peripheral vision, and you connect with someone on the same low-key, spacey level and engage in nondemanding but still relevant verbal communication about insights gained during the trip. Attempted too early, acid conversation is just a series of blips and verbal burps that may contain tremendous meaning to the burper, but are untranslatable to the listener.

When did you start walking toward the venue?

When did Shasta lock up the van?

Do you have your ticket?

Yes, you have your ticket.

Remember lining up to walk down the hall with your class in elementary school? Remember how everyone was supposed to stay in one neat line? But there were those giddy kids who just couldn't handle the restriction or control their bodies from bursting out into the middle of the corridor, or three kids down to pull the new girl's hair, or jumping into the air to swipe at the ceiling they have no hope of reaching? There were the kids nervous that the giddy kid would bring down the teacher's wrath on the whole class. There were the chatty kids. The blissfully vacant kids. The compulsively worried kids. The smart kids who wouldn't stop reading while they walked even though they regularly tripped over their untied shoelaces. There were the pretty kids. The thin, sickly kids. The kids from money. The kids with worn-out jeans and bad haircuts . . . .

Now get those kids fried on weed and LSD and tell them they're about to be turned loose in psychedelic Disneyland . . . .

Where's your ticket?

Is your weed hidden well enough to get past security?

Waiting on line to get into a Dead show, you are likely to feel like every one of those elementary school kids before you reach the entrance. You are giddy, nerdy, bashful, exhilarated, unabashedly compulsive . . . . Or you are surrounded by those kids and every time you look at one, you are pulled into that personality for an instant and become that kid . . . wait, these aren't kids, they are adults . . . . Is everyone as high as you? Where is your ticket? Is your weed hidden well enough? What will they open up with tonight? What are Shasta and Bart talking about? Sissy took off his Teva. Is his foot bleeding? Is your foot bleeding? Those Rainbow Heads are always looking for miracles . . . . Hope they get one . . . . Or is that just the sun in your eyes? Or is it cloudy? This mishmash of

*energies is unbearable and you have too much oxygen
and you are breathing heavy and too close to everyone,
bumping elbows, avoiding eyes—What will they open up
with?—you leap into the air and jig in place, you are
happier than you have ever been, you need to get inside
you need to get inside you need to explode to dance. . . .*

What will they open up with tonight?

*They took your ticket. You made it inside and they took
your ticket. You no longer have to worry about your
ticket. It's all good. No ticket worries. They didn't find
your weed either. Everyone made it inside. Hell, Kevin
even sneaked a little bong in down his pants.*

The hallway swirl.

*Shasta is leading the pack through the hallway. Spinners
are already twirling in the corners, their patchwork
dresses and dreadlocks carving out dance space on either
side of them. Non-tour-heads are lined up at the conces-
sion stands and GDP booths. They are spending money on
overpriced fatty food and beer. The smell of nachos and
hotdogs mixed with body odor, patchouli, weed smoke,
and stale beer spilled by metalheads at the Metallica
concert the week before, but you move through it fast,
Shasta knows how to slide through the hallway, you all*

do, you stay in formation, Shasta in front, then Sissy, then Bart, then you, then Harry, there is no need to talk, you are in a platoon of Deadhead soldiers, you are moving through the hallway on a mission to find the optimum hallway space that combines the best possible sound with plenty of room to move and similarly minded Deadheads with good, positive dance energy. You know there are hallway speakers at this venue. The sound will be best near the speakers (as opposed to loitering by an entrance ramp or open door where the sound isn't engineered to arrive), and the serious dancers will gather there—it will be a good crowd. You can already feel that. No one in your family is on a bum trip, and everyone had tickets for the show. Everyone is in. On the bus. You might poke your head inside the arena at some point. After you find your space in the hallway, you'll check out the orientation of the stage, see where everyone is set up and whether there are any changes to the gear onstage—you will close your eyes, lift up your head, breathe in the heavy air of expectation, allow the crisscrossing energy of thousands of jacked-up souls to enter your bloodstream through your lungs and fill your body.

Your family carves out space across the hallway from the speakers beside the ramp into the arena. The best spot. None of you needs to be inside the arena proper—as you say, you know what the band looks like, why bother? Here you can get the best sound from the speakers, maximize dance space, and have access to the inside of the arena in case the band breaks out something that needs to be witnessed with the eyes as well as the feet. You will also go inside the arena during "I Will Take You Home" because it's not much to dance to, and it's nice to see Brent in the spotlight. You will get high in there too. But not everyone ventures in at once because you would risk losing your key hallway position. Besides, you can always sneak a hit in the hallway. The arena security know as well as any Deadhead there—you have taken over the arena and the usual rules don't apply. The best arenas instruct their staff that Deadheads may be strange and even scary, but they're really harmless, peace-loving people. The Dead staff help them understand that. Deadheads will smoke pot. Don't worry about it. Just leave them alone, or you'll create more problems. Let them dance and act crazy, and it will all be fine.

You stretch your legs like you used to before soccer games. You touch the tips of your Converse All Stars. You swivel your waist. You rotate your neck and your whole body shivers inadvertently as a pent-up energy bubble pops and ricochets down your spine. You toss that energy out through your hands. Your hands. You learned at Dead shows how to dance with your hands. How to gather up balls of energy like packing snowballs and release them into the surrounding environment. You can touch other people with these balls of energy. You can make upset people feel better. You can alienate assholes who encroach into your dance territory until they're forced to go elsewhere. You can direct the music with them. You can direct your trip with them. You can act out the stalking swagger of a dire wolf; you can bop like Stagger Lee; you can plead with Althea; you can light fires on the mountain; you can strut out those walking blues; you can wave that flag. . . . Your hands, feet, and collective molecules learned how to dance at Dead shows, and it's the best thing you have ever done with your body.

The first wave of cheers hits when the lights in the arena go down. Some people charge from the hallway into the arena, but your family keeps their cool. You all move a little more. Kick your legs out to either side and try a few moves. Sissy hands you a packed one-hitter and a lighter. You crouch down, take a hit, stand up and exhale it into the hallway. People are smoking cigarettes everywhere anyway, so no one will notice another puff of smoke— not that anyone cares anyway. It smells delicious. The catcalls, whoops, whistles, and war cries stay steady through the first wave until the second wave crashes down engulfing the whole arena—the band is taking the stage. Brent slides casually onto his stool. Phil saunters out with a little grin and begins fiddling with his amp.

The drummers materialize behind their kits and make the first noise, tapping drum heads, rocking their feet on the kick drums. The largest applause is saved for Bobby and Jerry, who both give little waves as they enter the stage and adjust their guitar straps across their shoulders. The notes come sliding out of the sound system. Brent pushes down the keys and a whir swirls down your cochlea expanding into warm chocolate behind your eyes. Jerry does a few runs down the neck sending sparkler streams across the arena. Phil drops a couple big, fat notes, then pulls up high onto the neck sending goose bumps down your forearms. The drummers tap, roll, ride their cymbal bells, cueing your feet into the joy they're about to experience. You can't help yourself. You dash up the ramp into the arena and check out the band. Bobby's hair is long now and pulled back into a ponytail. Jerry is looking fit (for Jerry anyway) and wearing his trademark black T-shirt. Phil is sporting a garish tie-dye on his pear-shaped torso. Brent is shifting his narrow shoulders on his piano stool, trying to get situated, eyeing the lineup across the stage—Jerry, Bobby, Phil—for cues about what will happen next. The drummers are saying something to each other: Bill is chuckling and Mickey is grinning like the devil holding a full house. You rotate slowly to take in the full 360-degree view of the arena. Lights out. Lighters sparking up everywhere—tiny pinpricks in the sky. The crowd is chattering, howling, calling out band members'

*names, song titles, yelling "We love you" and making it
sound like they mean more than just the band, they love it
all, everyone and everything that's going on in the arena.
You feel a little off-balance by the sheer energy. Every
available corner is filled with Deadheads with enormous
pupils and stupid grins. They are in their favorite place in
the world. They are ready to dance. To hear what the
band has to give them and to give it right back to the
band. There are also random straight people in the
crowd—parents who got dragged in by their kids, or baby
boomers on a nostalgia trip, or just locals with a healthy
curiosity—and they are the fun ones to watch. They have
never seen anything like this. The hippies. The smells. The
expectation. The adoration. The dancing. The strange,
chattering behavior. They are alternately amused or terrified, but they aren't ever bored. They will take something
away from the night. We all will.*

What will they open up with?

*Deadheads have speculated on this all day. What will they
open the show with? What will they play? What have
they already played this tour, and what haven't they
broken out since the West Coast? What are the rumors?
"Alligator"? "Mason's Children"? There are always the
rumors that they sound-checked "St. Stephen" somewhere
and someone heard they were going to break it out. It is*

pre-Hampton 10.9.89, so "Dark Star" is just a dream leftover from 1984, but still a dream that gets raised in speculation before every show.

What will they open up with?

You sway back down the ramp into the hallway and slide in next to Shasta. He's moving and looking at his feet. The hallway isn't crowded—you all have plenty of room. The notes are coming more regularly now—Jerry, then Phil, then Mickey, then Jerry, then Brent, then Bill, then Bobby—and they are beginning to sync up. To communicate. They are beginning to shape themselves into their first form. The song that will kick off the show. That will set your body moving. That will dictate your first groove. Bart takes a bat hit and hands it back to Sissy, who slides it into the side pocket of his army pants. Harry lets out a little whoop and jumps up and down in place. We are all grinning like lucky fools. The notes are coming together into one of your favorite openers: the funky, weird, good-dancing, true-lyric opener that sets the vibe for the whole evening and sums up the anticipation at the start of a Dead show better than any other: "Feel Like A Stranger":

> *Inside you're burning*
> *I can see clear through*
> *Your eyes tell more than you mean them to*
> *Lit up and flashing*

Like the reds and blues
Out there on the neon avenue

There was a time when this song laid you flat out on the
floor of the Oakland Coliseum. But not this time. You
have grown into the song, the scene, and now it is yours.
Your family is dancing together. This is a killer opener,
harbinger of an outstanding night to come. You shake
your hands, your hair, you are smiling at each other in
ways that no one outside of this experience will ever see—
the true joy, the body movement, the brotherhood of your
family united under the Grateful Dead creates a bond you
will always share no matter how far apart you drift.
There are beautiful Deadhead girls dancing in the hall-
way too. Their skirts are billowing out as they spin. Their
bodies are lithe, sexy, hairy, fascinatingly pungent, erotic,
expressive, evocative—echoing every note, lyric, and
improvisation the band blows out. You are not hitting on
them. This is a safe space for them and for you. It is a
creative space—you would never dance so freely in front
of the girls from your high school. Or the boys for that
matter. But here, among your family, you are safe to
express yourself in dance. It is understood. The music
would have nothing less. There is an old hippie in tie-dyed
long underwear across the hallway with a smile spread
beyond the confines of his face. There is an awkward,
acne-covered teenage girl in a velvet dress that's too

heavy for dancing. There is a tawny, tanned, long-haired dude you just know is from the West Coast. You can tell it by his skin, by the way he moves, and you know that in the moment of the song there is no such thing as coasts. Stragglers are still making their way through the hallway on their way in to find their seats in the arena—they inadvertently pass through the hallway dancers and are simultaneously absorbed, embraced, and allowed and encouraged to move through so that they don't overburden your good scene and they find their way wherever they need to go. They could join the hallway, but only if they do it seamlessly. Only if they dance into the scene already united with the vibe of the dancers. No one wants a space invader fucking up the vibe. It's not personal. Just what's happening at the moment. And what's happening at the moment isn't about being polite. It's about music, dancing, ritual, family, exploration. And it's going to be a long, long crazy, crazy night . . . .

Once a Prankster, Always a Prankster

You're either on the bus or off the bus.

—Merry Prankster Motto

Every society reveres some sort of trickster figure. Carl Jung summed up the archetypal trickster as, "a primitive cosmic being of divine-animal nature, on the one-hand superior to man because of his supernatural qualities, and on the other inferior to him because of his unreason and unconsciousness." Whether it is the West African spider trickster Anansi who, through trickery and misdirection, turned an ear of corn into one hundred slaves, or the beloved American Bugs Bunny, always tweaking the powers-that-be with a twitch of his whiskers and percussive snicker, we love the trickster who outwits while imparting lessons that can be passed on for generations.

The culture surrounding the Grateful Dead is no different. Each founding member of the Grateful Dead came to the band after being driven out of—and consciously detaching from—mainstream society. They were outsiders as individuals before joining the band. Those same traits that made them outsiders bonded them together, allowing them to become, collectively, some of the best pranksters this country has ever seen.

Pigpen

Ron "Pigpen" McKernan was the son of a boogie-woogie piano player turned rhythm-and-blues disc jockey who broadcasted under the moniker "Cool Breeze." His father's musical tastes rubbed off quickly on young Ron. By the time he was sixteen, Pigpen had a deep knowledge of the lineage of the blues, its players, and the labels that specialized in recording them. He claimed to have started drinking at twelve years old and by all accounts, that seems likely. He wore dirty jeans and T-shirts, had long greasy hair, and a motorcycle chain around his wrist. One of his closest friends as a teenager was an older black man named Tawny Jones.

Tawny owned a Harley Davidson and knew where to buy bootleg whiskey in La Honda for $1.50 a gallon. But, most importantly, Tawny introduced Pigpen to places like the Anchor Club and Popeye Club in East Palo Alto and the Aztec Lounge in San Mateo, where the teenage blues aficionado soaked up authentic blues, and plenty of booze. He was a weird-looking white kid in a predominantly black blues bar. He wrote poetry, painted, read science fiction, played piano, and looked like grease-and-leather hell on earth; a white teenager hanging out and drinking whiskey with black blues musicians at a charged moment in America when it came to racial integration of any kind. Pigpen was kicked out of Palo Alto High School before he could graduate, but one suspects that his education was utterly unimpeded.

Jerry

Jerome John Garcia was born in San Francisco in 1942. His father was a Spanish immigrant who played in and conducted swing bands. In 1947, Jerry lost his father in a drowning accident that Garcia is on record as having witnessed and remembered. Also in 1947, Jerry lost the top two joints of the middle finger on his right hand in a wood chopping accident. As a boy he showed an early acuity for visual art and a passion for music and reading. In 1957, Jerry discovered guitar, cigarettes, and marijuana: the gateways to a bohemian future were thrown wide open. By the time the Warlocks—the early incarnation of the Grateful Dead—played their first gig together in 1964 at a pizza parlor in Menlo Park, Jerry was already a husband and father. However, he had also been discharged from the army for being AWOL so many times. Simply put, Jerry's priorities lay not with military duty, nor with family responsibilities, but with absorbing San Francisco's folk scene, which at that time was still buzzing with Beat energy. The alternative lifestyles of that folk scene, in which Jerry would become a major figure, would morph into hippie society a few short, turbulent years later. And Jerry Garcia would benignly lead that parade, guitar in hand.

Phil

In 1944, after recognizing that the four-year-old Philip Lesh was already exhibiting a passion for classical music, Phil's grandmother took him to hear his first symphony. From that point on, Phil's obvious intelligence combined with his enchantment with music to create a singular personality, driven to perfection. His hard work, artistic prowess, and high IQ would allow him to excel in school music programs. But those same traits solidified him as an outsider among his peers. In today's parlance, Lesh might be called a Band Geek. But he was a band geek who fell under the spell of the Beat poets, cool jazz musicians, marijuana, avant-garde composers such as John Cage, and, eventually, his hip bosom buddy, Jerry Garcia.

Bobby

Today's parlance has many terms for Bob Weir too. An undiagnosed dyslexic with a wiseass streak raised in an upper middle-class family; a good-looking but spacey kid more interested in hanging out with his friends, partying, and playing music than attending to his studies: Bob Weir was the prototypical suburban slacker. Of all the Dead band members, Weir is the one who would've fit in immediately with my own group of high school friends. He was smart, but not in a way that served him at all in the straight world. He got the girls because he was so damn pretty, not because he tried too hard to get them. He was charismatic in the way of all class clowns. At one point, this slacker attitude got him kicked out of the Grateful Dead, but Bob simply didn't leave.

Billy

Bill Kreutzman was born in 1946, and among his earliest memories is playing drums for a dance class his mother taught at Stanford University. As with all the band members, it seems that Bill was born to play his instrument. His early exposure to drums and his dedication to mastering them set him on an early path that would distinguish him as one of the Bay Area's top young drummers. This early passion also set him firmly outside the concerns of his mainstream peers and perhaps heightened his taste for alternative lifestyles, viewpoints, and outsider personalities. In eighth grade, Bill found a drumming and lifestyle mentor in Stanford grad student named Lee Anderson. Anderson, a physics student, gave Bill drum lessons, but also introduced him to altered states (via extravagant mixed drinks) and to the bohemian dancers, artists, and writers—including a creative writing student named Ken Kesey—who were Anderson's friends. When he was a teenager, Bill's parents divorced after years of fighting. To get him out of a tumultuous home environment, Bill was sent to the Orme School in Arizona. He hated it there, until his drums were sent out to him. There is a wonderful story about Bill practicing his drums in the auditorium of the Orme School when the headmaster appeared and asked him to stop—the guest speaker for the night's presentation had arrived. The speaker, however, asked Bill to continue playing so that he could listen. That speaker was Aldous Huxley. His lecture for the evening would focus on psychedelic drugs and their historic impact and potential implications on society.

Mickey

Mickey Hart, too, was a born drummer. In fact, both his parents were drummers—a large part of their courting process involved playing together. Mickey's father, Lenny Hart, was named the world senior solo rudimental drum champion at the 1939 New York World's Fair. His mother, Leah, joined Lenny at the fair to win the world mixed-doubles championship. Unfortunately, Lenny would desert the family soon after Mickey was born, leaving the boy to be raised by his mother and her subsequent husbands. Mickey never clicked with his stepfathers. He was often on his own and found solace in the drums that seemed his birthright. In his own words, from the age of ten, "all I did was drum. Obsessively. Passionately. Painfully." Lenny would resurface in Mickey's life at different times, and never fail to disappoint—or blatantly rip off—his son. The final straw was when Lenny served as the Grateful Dead's financial manager in the late 60s. Lenny eventually bilked the band for roughly $155,000 before skipping town. Mickey was devastated, of course, but his new alternative family—the Grateful Dead—rallied around him.

The individuals who formed the original core of the Grateful Dead came into the situation as outsiders, agitators, and tricksters. But despite Pigpen's unfortunate nickname (which was derived from the *Peanuts* comic strip, home of another famous American trickster, Snoopy) the members of the Grateful Dead were not animals, as is the case with tricksters throughout history. They were human. Thus, they weren't really tricksters after all. They were freaks, a label they eagerly embraced, an affront to the very forces who used the terms oppressively. These freaks dressed funny, talked funny, acted funny . . . . Their whole culture was set up as a snub to mainstream society. They dressed like Victorian dandies in an era of flat tops and khakis. They wore feather boas, coonskin caps, top hats, sashes, elfin shoes, riverboat gambler garb, dashikis, you name it. They played Motown hits at ungodly volume while high on acid. The mistake that most people make is to imagine the members of the Grateful Dead as peace-love-and-flower-touting hippies. They were not. They were more likely to mess with your mind than to soothe it. In short—even before they merged their scene with Ken Kesey's in the mid-60s—they were pranksters. Ken Kesey just made it official. He formally introduced the figure of The Prankster, the human-striving-toward-superhuman version of The Trickster, into Grateful Dead culture.

Ken Kesey and the Merry Pranksters could easily be called the first Deadheads.

In 1959, while Ken Kesey was a graduate student studying creative writing through a Woodrow Wilson Fellowship at Stanford University, he volunteered to take part in a government drug research program being conducted at Menlo Park Veterans Hospital. As it turned out, the drugs were psychedelics: LSD, mescaline, psilocybin, and amphetamine IT-290. Prior to those research tests, Kesey had already begun his transformation from country boy athlete (a wrestler while at The University of Oregon, he was admitted to the Stanford Writing Program based on a football-themed novel he was working on) to psychedelic prankster. With his wife Faye, Kesey was living in the bohemian section of Palo Alto. He had grown a beard, started playing folk guitar, had his senses rearranged by pot brownies and booze, and had begun hanging out at a North Beach coffee house called The Place where poets and street philosophers were provided with solemn, attentive audiences. Future Merry Pranksters such as Jane Burton, Ed McClanahan, and Ken Babbs were among Kesey's friends living on Perry Lane in Palo Alto at that time.

As Kesey's social and intellectual circles were being widened by Stanford and his new bohemian lifestyle, the MK-ULTRA program—courtesy of the CIA—would come along and turn Kesey onto psychedelics. Kesey heard about the local MK-ULTRA program through his friend Vic Lovell, who was a psychology student at the time. The program Kesey signed up for was being run by Dr. Leo Hollister at the Veterans Hospital in Menlo Park. For $100 in pay, subjects would allow themselves to be dosed with psychedelics and then studied, questioned, and run through various tests by researchers. Even though Kesey wasn't crazy about every drug he was given, he gained a quick affinity for the LSD. In a 1964 interview for the Bay Area newspaper the *Peninsula Times Tribune*, Kesey said, "With these drugs, your perception is altered enough that you find yourself looking out of completely strange eyeholes. All of us have a great deal of our minds locked shut. And these drugs seem to be the key to open these locked doors."

By his words and experiences, Kesey was closely mirroring those of Aldous Huxley, who had volunteered for psychedelic research in 1953. Huxley's experience with LSD was no less revelatory, and had led him to write the book *The Doors of Perception*, in which he states, "But the man who comes back through the Door in the Wall will never be quite the same as the man who went out. He will be wiser but less cocksure, happier but less self-satisfied, humbler in acknowledging his ignorance yet better equipped to understand the relationship of words to things, of systematic reasoning to the unfathomable Mystery which it tries, forever vainly, to comprehend."

But perhaps visionary poet and artist William Blake said it truest and clearest: "If the doors of perception were cleansed everything would appear to man as it is, infinite."

Jim Morrison liked this "doors of perception" idea so much that he shortened it and named his band after it: The Doors.

Regardless of the high-brow literary and medical pedigree of LSD, Kesey was about to bring it down to street level. As the Menlo Park MK-ULTRA tests proceeded in clinical settings, samples of LSD began turning up among Kesey's friends in Perry Lane. Here Kesey and his friends—many of whom would form the core of the Merry Pranksters—began the serious play of LSD experimentation. They were miles away from the CIA-appointed lab tests at the Veterans Hospital, or the various MK-ULTRA CIA tests that witnessed unwitting soldiers, military scientists, and average citizens being dosed and observed, often to heinous— even fatal—ends. They were also miles away from the psychological, intellectual, and spiritual investigations being undertaken under the auspices of Dr. Timothy Leary and Dr. Richard Alpert's psychedelic tests at Harvard University. In short, Kesey and his friends

were hanging out together and mixing LSD with
bohemian activities—music, art, writing, sex, passionate
discussions about politics and philosophy, etc.—to
create their own burgeoning proto-hippie scene.

During the time all this Perry Lane dosing was going
on, Kesey decided to take a summer job as a psychiatric
aide at the Veterans Hospital. It kept him close to his
psychedelic source, plus gave him time—and a great
deal of subject matter—for the new book he was
working on, *One Flew Over the Cuckoo's Nest*. The book
would center around a Native American mental patient,
Chief Bromden, and his struggle against society's (in
the form of the hospital) impulse to destroy individuality, and, in turn, the individual. Between the things he
saw (sometimes while tripping-on-the-job) at the Veterans Hospital, his own bohemian training, and his
sharpened writing chops, Kesey turned out a literary
masterpiece of antiestablishment fiction. When the
book was published in 1962, Kesey became the classic
literary Wonderboy, an overnight success, receiving
thoughtful reviews in, among other places, the *New
York Times*, the *Saturday Review*, and *Time* magazine.
Kesey had become a national celebrity.

Not only did the critical and commercial success of
One Flew Over the Cuckoo's Nest lay the groundwork for
Kesey's writing career, but it allowed him the financial
freedom to buy property out in the country, in La

Honda, California. Kesey moved to La Honda in 1963, and his lively, tripping gang of Perry Lane friends followed him there. La Honda would become the base camp of the Merry Pranksters. It was from La Honda that the Prankster's famous acid-soaked, cross-country bus trip in a 1939 International Harvester school bus would be organized. Although the first official acid tests were held at various locations, not directly at La Honda, the property—filled with tripping freaks, art, music, and speakers hidden in the trees to broadcast disorienting random speech and noises—could fairly be described as a geographically fixed, perpetual acid test.

Among this band of Merry Pranksters was the iconographic literary figure Neal Cassady, the hero of Jack Kerouac's zeitgeist-setting novel, *On the Road*. Shortly after Neal had returned from driving the Prankster's bus—Furthur—cross-country (inspiring Bob Weir's climactic lyrics in "The Other One," "There was Cowboy Neal at the wheel, the bus to Never-Never Land"), he was hanging out in St. Michael's Alley in Palo Alto when he invited a young woman named Carolyn Adams to smoke a joint with him. Neal and Carolyn hit it off immediately, so Neal took her back to La Honda and introduced her around to the Pranksters. That woman soon became a core Prankster, earning the Prankster moniker, Mountain Girl. Mountain Girl would, in turn, become Jerry Garcia's second wife.

In *The Grateful Dead Family Album* Jerry Garcia described the personal and musical freedom of playing at the Acid Tests this way: "The nice thing about the Acid Test was that we could play or not. And a lot of times we'd really be too high to play, and we'd play for maybe a *minute* and then we'd lose it and have to leave—'This it too weird for me!' On the other hand, sometimes we'd play and there was no pressure on us because people didn't come to see the Grateful Dead, they came for the Acid Test; it was the whole event that counted. Therefore we weren't in the spotlight, so when we did play, we played with a certain kind of freedom you rarely get as a musician. Not only did we not have to fulfill expectations about us, we didn't have to fulfill expectations about *music*, either. So in terms of being able to experiment freely with music, it was amazing."

Garcia would himself become extremely burdened by the expectations and demands associated with being the supposed leader of the Grateful Dead. Toward the end of this life, he sought musical escape by returning to the folk songs and sea chanteys of his youth through collaborations with mandolin player David Grisman and others. Of course, he also sought escape, solace, friendship, and—decreasingly—new frontiers through drug use his entire adult life. But aside from musical genius, Garcia was a flat-out, dyed-in-the-wool, freedom-loving freak, and always the prankster. The Acid Tests may have allowed Garcia to temporarily escape himself, but they also created the blueprint for the Grateful Dead shows that would dominate the rest of his life.

Of course, being born in 1970, I was nowhere near an original Acid Test. Still, for Deadheads interested not only in the music, but in the cultural importance of the band (and, make no mistake, every Deadhead is an amateur historian), the spirit of the Acid Tests was a powerful touchstone. The history of the Merry Pranksters is our history. Ken Kesey was, in many ways, the founding father of all Deadheads. And for Deadheads who were true believers in the artistic, spiritual, intellectual, psychic, and playful potentialities of mixing hallucinogens and music in a space where wild behavior was not only expected, but encouraged, the Acid Tests never really stopped. They were revived every time the Grateful Dead rolled into town. Indeed, many who have attended one or two Grateful Dead concerts will recount the shows with awe, never once mentioning the band. That's because these people attended a Dead show, not just a concert by a band called the Grateful Dead. In a very real way, what they had attended was a contemporary version of the 1960s Acid Test.

I am a Deadhead because I love the music of the Grateful Dead. I learned the joy of the prankster and the freedom of the freak by going deep enough into Dead culture to surpass being an observer at Dead shows, or even a Grateful Dead fan, and becoming a freak who helped shape other people's experiences.

It was 1989, and my friend Harry and I were on East Coast spring tour. I was eighteen years old and saddled with troubling acne. As we would on several tours, we were traveling together in Shasta's green VW bus. By this time Shasta wasn't as big of an acid-head as Harry and I, which was for the best because he was more able to navigate crowded parking lots to get us on the road to the next show immediately after the previous night's show had ended. At any given point of a Dead show the three of us could be scattered at completely different parts of the venue. Sometimes we went into a show together. Sometimes we went in on our own. We all knew different people and, on any given night, had different ideas about how we wanted to experience the show. By spring tour 1989, I had been to more than a dozen shows and was as comfortable as you can be taking an unpredictable drug like LSD in a crowd of a few thousand people.

On this particular night, Harry and I had ended up in the same place when the final note died out, so we made our way out into the parking lot together along with the rest of the herd. On this night, we were both on top of our trips and in similar psychic spaces. We were elated and playful: teenage Deadheads far from home. Harry and I were good friends from high school; we had graduated together the spring before and had bonded hard over drugs and the Grateful Dead the past couple of years. We called each other "family" without a speck of irony. My curly hair had grown from afro to dangling corkscrew curls mixed with dreadlocks. Harry had long, greasy blond hair and was a snuffed roach of a kid. Between the crappy road food and lack of hygiene, my acne—which, as with most self-conscious teenagers, was a source of acute embarrassment—was going through a major flare-up.

But for the first time since adolescence, I didn't care.

Despite the drugs and years since, I remember with amazing clarity the feeling of exiting that show with Harry. I was high as hell, absolutely flying, on acid. I had a massive white-head zit right between my eyes. As usual, there were stoned locals being stupid everywhere. This was the peak of the Touch of Grey era, so more than ever before in the band's history, there were straight-laced civilians mixed in with Heads. In other words: people to fuck with. Harry and I were pranksters. We were Deadheads. We were freaks. We were standing close behind wigged-out straight people talking to each other in speedy gibberish, pretending that the conversation made perfect sense. We were dancing, singing, swinging our arms like drowning pixies in a vat of mushroom tea. We were standing among hundreds of crunchy, politically-correct-striving hippies and we were yelling, "Yummy Spam Stir-Fry! Two bucks, what the fuck!" just to see who it would mess with. And whenever we'd get someone, whenever they'd turn to see who these loud-mouths were, I'd point to the massive, puss-filled, white-capped zit on my forehead and say, "Third eye."

Perhaps this is all juvenile. In the larger sense, there is nothing revolutionary about fucking with stoned people's minds. But consider this: I had been incredibly self-conscious about my acne ever since I entered adolescence. There were many days I didn't want to go to school because of how my face looked. As with most teens, I imagined that the physical trait I was least secure about was the only thing that people noticed about me. Yet here I was, not only unembarrassed by my acne, but pointing it out to people. My peers even. I didn't give a fuck about being cool. I was a freak. My acne was my freak flag. And Harry—my brother Dead-head, my family—thought it was absolutely beautiful and hilarious that I was using my zit to mess with people. In America, particularly among teens, acne is meant to be hidden. Although it was certainly not intellectualized this way at the time (just knowing that we were "messing with people's minds" was enough),

I was forcing these people to confront their notions of beauty and acceptance. I had the big zit; I was a smelly, hairy freak; and I was absolutely in control of this space, this isolated encounter. I had also assimilated hippie subculture enough to reference the Hindu concept of the third eye in my prank. But, personally, any effect I may have had on other people's thinking that night is overshadowed by the understanding of what I confronted on a personal level to pull such a prank.

LSD forces you to deal with your insecurities like a matador squaring off against a bull with its nuts in a noose. How you handle those insecurities can often mean the difference between a good trip that actually increases your awareness of the world, and a horrifying trip that can mentally scar you for life. When—again as part of their top secret MK-ULTRA program—CIA officials dosed a group of CIA personnel at a work conference in Maryland, they did not realize how serious those mental scars can be. Dr. Frank Olson, a biological warfare researcher who was covertly dosed in Maryland, ended, in the words of Columbia University LSD researcher Dr. Harold Abramson, who examined Olson, trapped in "a psychotic state . . . with delusions of persecution . . . crystallized by the LSD experience."

Soon after, Dr. Frank Olson would commit suicide by jumping from the tenth-story window of a Manhattan hotel.

On the other end, any seasoned tripper will tell you that every time you take LSD you are confronted with a familiar world made strange and fascinating. Albert Hofmann, who accidentally created and ingested LSD on April 16, 1943, while trying to develop a cure for migraine headaches, recorded the first acid trip as such: "[What overcame me was] a remarkable but not unpleasant state of intoxication . . . characterized by an intense stimulation of the imagination, an altered state of awareness of the world. As I lay in a dazed condition with eyes closed there surged up from me a succession of fantastic, rapidly changing imagery of a striking reality and depth, alternating with a vivid, kaleidoscopic play of colors."

Ken Kesey, reflecting an additional two decades of LSD "research" and certainly with more literary flair, reported, "I've found psychedelics to be keys to worlds that have always existed, that have to be talked about. The kaleidoscopic pictures, the geometrics of humanity, that one experiences under, say, mescaline, aren't concealed in the white crystals inside the gelatin capsule. They are always in the mind. In the world. Already. The chemical allows the picture to be seen. To know the world you need to see as many sides of it as possible. And this sometimes means using microscopes, telescopes, spectroscopes, even kaleidoscopes. . . . Drugs didn't create those descriptions any more than Joyce's eyeglasses created *Ulysses*. They merely help one to see the paper more clearly."

LSD can turn the world into a kaleidoscope, yes, but it can also force you to stare down your insecurities and learn things about yourself that people who have never tripped will never get to learn. LSD is a club. The dues can be a bitch. In my memory, I wear the experience of turning the prior shame of my acne into a dynamic prankster routine—the fact that I stared down this physical insecurity to the point that I made it into a strength—like some kind of psychedelic graduation ring. That was my opportunity to "pass the acid test."

Of course, I'm still as rife with insecurities as anyone. In fact, there are times that I'm sure those insecurities are even amplified due to heavy use of psychedelics during my teens. Times when a look in the mirror gives a disembodied effect similar to staring into one's own dilated pupils while peaking in the bathroom of a funeral parlor (no, I never did). One of the problems with teenage drug abuse is that you never get to know what your adult brain would be like without it. Am I more insecure, more unstable, more anxious or depressed, as a result of dropping all that acid at Dead shows (and parks, and parties, and school, and . . .)? I don't know. I can't know. But I do know that the lessons I learned while touring with the Grateful Dead are the most valuable and formative of my life. I also know that staring into some of those terrifying abysses while high on acid taught me how to soothe myself in moments of extreme psychic—and physical—distress.

When I was seventeen years old, I started to experience excruciating pain in my lower spine region on a regular basis. The sensation was a combination burning, cramping, stabbing pain that always struck at night. It drove me into twisting convulsions in an attempt to find a position that would alleviate the pain. Some positions worked. Placing my feet above my head with a fist balled up and jammed into the lower left side of my back, just below my ribcage, helped a little. But nothing made the pain go away. I made a couple of trips to the emergency room during this period. I went to doctors. I got X-rays. I was usually given something to alleviate gas or other gastrointestinal problems. I was told not to eat greasy food. I was told it was all in my head. These problems persisted, undiagnosed, for three years. Until finally, one night at college in Potsdam, I started pissing blood.

My diagnosis was uretero-pelvic junction (or UPJ) obstruction. My urologist also called it "beer-itis" because it tends to make itself known when people go to college and binge drink (I didn't bother telling him that I had gotten started on that process a little earlier than most). The bottom line was that there was an obstruction in my ureter between the kidney and the bladder (in my case, a blood vessel), so that the kidney couldn't excrete the urine as well as it should. So it swelled. The more I drank, the more my kidney swelled, the worse the pain got. At times, my pain was often so unbearable I came close to passing out.

Basically, my kidney had been intermittently swelling to the point of rupturing.

Eventually I underwent an operation to clear the blockage. By that time, I'd lost partial use of my left kidney but, thankfully, not a total loss of function. Unsurprisingly, the entire experience—the years of pain, as well as the operation (not laproscopic, unfortunately) and recovery—is heavily intertwined with my Dead touring experience. At first it might sound strange that I never experienced the pain while on tour. But aside from a few beers here and there, I didn't drink on tour. I smoked pot and took psychedelics. And somewhere along the way the mental training of dealing with acid trips also overlapped with the physical and mental struggle of dealing with this agonizing pain. Without any coaching, I learned to focus on my breathing. I was practicing meditation without a name for it. I breathed to get me through the personal psychic darkness that sometimes erupts out of a particularly intense acid trip. I breathed to get me through the very real physical pain that haunted my nights for years. I visualized, I breathed, and I got through some dark fucking spaces. And when I finally underwent the operation to correct my condition, I breathed through the recovery and the various painful procedures and indignities—including a second emergency operation to remove a broken drainage tube from my body—and I tried to get stronger. Because the truth is that inside of every prankster, particularly the psychedelic kind, there is also a warrior.

Fire on
the Mountain

Not all warriors survive the battle.

DEADHEAD DETECTIVES HAVE
LOTS OF TICKETS

Albany Times Union, March 28, 1993

by Donna Liquori

ALBANY—Tie dyes? Check. Bandanas?
Check. Beads? Check. Wristwatch? No,
not quite.

Narcotics detectives going undercover
Saturday amid the influx of Grateful
Dead fans warned their supervisor,

Detective Sgt. Tom Fitzpatrick, that the watch would be, well, a dead giveaway.

Deadheads really couldn't care less what time it was, the detectives warned him.

Fitzpatrick, wearing a white woven sweatshirt of the kind Deadheads covet, said he knew that and would ditch the watch before he hit the streets surrounding the Knickerbocker Arena.

By 1 p.m., a Psychedelic throng wandered around the roads, some enjoying the scene, others trying to buy tickets. The investigator's job was to blend in and fool the ones with the drugs.

But getting arrested isn't exactly a bad thing for Deadheads. "It's part of being a Deadhead," Detective Jim Lyman said. "It's a status symbol."

Lyman, wearing sunglasses, a multicolored hat, a beaded bag, ripped jeans and another one of those weaved pullovers, practiced acting Dead by holding up his finger, saying, "I need a miracle," the phrase used by the Dead's faithful when seeking a ticket for a sold-out concert.

Everyone in the special investigations unit is anxious to work when the Grateful Dead come to town. It's their Halloween.

Even the desk officer, Detective Daniel Ryan, sported a multicolored beanie.

And arresting the concert goers doesn't come with all the hassles accompanying other drug suspects. They're generally more mellow.

"Basically, they're the nicest people in the world to arrest," Lyman said.

And they're also good learning tools. Fitzpatrick said the investigators learn the latest in drug paraphernalia and types of drugs available. The investigators came across liquid LSD when the hippie-emulating crowd was in town.

A talkative Deadhead will provide the unit with "street intelligence" to make their jobs easier, particularly when they're searching for drugs that aren't the normal drugs of choice in Albany.

"We don't do a lot of LSD," Fitzpatrick said, meaning, of course, arrests. "It's inherent to them."

Fitzpatrick spoke on the second floor of Division 2, police headquarters. A small group of cops dressed rather convincingly in tie dyed T-shirts hung out in the hall, urging Fitzpatrick to hurry. One came in and popped a rainbow colored hat on Fitzpatrick's graying hair.

The sergeant admits he gets "made" by Deadheads pretty easily. The Deadheads will slap a sticker on undercover officers once they're discovered. So he lets others in the unit make the buys. Fitzpatrick said most of those arrested only care about one thing: getting out of jail in time for the concert. Often, police will accommodate them with tickets—court appearance tickets, that is.

As the police Deadheads made their way to the Knick, one person asked for directions, another honked, and one man, not a Deadhead, recognized them and shouted out a few profanities for their undercover looks.

Once in the general area of the Knick,
they mingled freely, buying food and
checking out the wares for sale in the
parking lot (that's where they buy
their costumes).

Clothes and drugs were not the only
things people were looking to buy.
Concert tickets were at a premium.

"We tried to order them. We came down
and are hoping for the best," said Zack
Belcher, a college student from Boston
as he sat cross-legged on the sidewalk
along South Pearl Street.

Courtney, just Courtney, from
Saratoga, peddled oranges out of a
knapsack for 50 cents each. "Most
people buy oranges to trip. You eat,
then you go zing," she said. Courtney,
also ticketless, drove down to hang out
with the thousands of fans. "It's an
awesome day."

Matt Aucon of New Hampshire sold canes
that were actually pipes. "It's kind of
unobvious," he said. He demonstrated by
pulling the plugs out of the top and
bottom of the black cane decorated with
dancing skeletons. He sucked in on the

bottom, and someone walking past yelled,

"That's a pretty long hit, man."

He didn't seem too disappointed about not selling any. He had three tickets. "All three nights. I'm psyched."

45 DRUG ARRESTS LINKED TO CONCERT

ALBANY—By midnight Saturday city police officers made 45 drug related arrests, many of them felonies, in the wake of the first of three Grateful Dead concerts at the Knickerbocker Arena.

One of those arrested, 20-year-old Jonathan Welsh of Jay, Maine, is facing four felony counts after allegedly possessing 344 hits of the hallucinogenic drug LSD.

"We made numerous arrests. We're talking 45, a lot of serious felonies," said an Albany police officer who declined to give his name. "A lot of uniforms (uniformed officers) made arrests. It's right out in the open."

The officer said the arrest total does not include those made by other police agencies. City police said more than

```
1,000 hits of hallucinogenic drugs had
been confiscated. "They're making 50
cents on the dollar. They're facing 15
to 20 years in jail," the officer said.
"They didn't use their heads."
```

I never went to prison. None of my friends ever did. They went to jail, yes, but never prison. But many Deadheads got prison sentences for drugs that were such a part of their culture that the busts themselves seemed like a farce. Indeed, the busts might have—at first—seemed less important even than getting into the show. But, as the "Before" and "After" nature of the above articles illustrates, the party could quickly come to a crashing halt. The police in every city knew damn well that they could rack up busts when the Dead came to town. Dress up in silly clothes. Bust kids as peaceful as sunflower seeds. No fights, no tensions, no risk of assault, half the time the Deadheads didn't even realize they were getting busted until they were shut into the silvery rear of some cop van. The Grateful Dead were bait. Merchants around the shows jacked up their prices on food and water. Hotels doubled their rates— and were still filled to capacity. Dazed hippies disassociated from the straight reality of locals wandered everywhere, lost, stranded, hoping for the best.

They were easy pickings.

My friend Harry hanged himself dead from a tree in Durango, Colorado, when he was twenty-one years old. He didn't hang himself because of drugs or any experiences related to the Grateful Dead. I would argue that he only stuck around the planet as long as he did because of the Grateful Dead. Growing up, his stepfather knocked him down—punched him out, kicked him, beat him up—and his mother didn't do much of anything to stop it. He had a little sister whom he adored but couldn't protect. Besides, Harry got the worst of it. Perhaps, as with many protective older siblings in his position, he drew the beatings away from her and onto himself. Either way, Harry got the brunt of his stepfather's aggression. So, like many teenage Deadheads, finding the Grateful Dead and the community that surrounded the band offered Harry the most substantial support system he'd had.

Early on, pre–Grateful Dead, when my favorite band was still Pink Floyd, Harry's main band was The Doors. He idolized Jim Morrison and often carried around Doors lyrics copied out in blue ink onto torn pages of notebook paper. In retrospect, it fascinates me how a kid like Harry—hell, a kid like me—who wouldn't have opened a school book if there was a twenty dollar bill inside (well, maybe. . . . That was the price of an eighth of weed back in 1988) would instead spend hours poring over lyrics, fascinated by the poetic imagery, relating the song concepts of their favorite lyricists to their own lives. We didn't just read the lyrics—we studied those lyrics. It was the only thing we studied.

One day Harry pulled out the lyrics to Morrison's "The End" in the parking lot of our high school. His stepfather had beaten him up pretty badly the night before. He was tripping. He was crying. He was telling me he was going to kill himself, and I believed him. He wouldn't kill himself that day, as it turns out, but Harry was telling the truth. Now there is no way that I could justify LSD as helping Harry's situation in this case. Other than illustrating that someone else felt as forsaken and hopeless as him ("This is the end, my only friend, the end"), it's doubtful that Morrison's lyrics did him any good either. But I do like to tell myself that having me to talk to that day helped Harry. I tell myself that the fact that I ditched school to wander around the woods and the trestle during his trip helped him get through that day (like a good boy, as the year went on, I even brought our favorite teacher into the situation, and he helped Harry in his own adult way). And when Harry and I started going to Dead shows together—that support system grew for him. He had more people to talk to about the song lyrics he loved. He found out that it was okay—it was fucking unbelievable—to dance like you were possessed by animal spirits. He found out that there were all sorts of screwed-up people in the world who had been through bad shit and could relate to his situation.

He also learned there were those who were eager to prey on people like him. And cops willing to throw him in jail for the drugs he escaped into. With the Grateful Dead, it's never all about peace, love, and family. It's always yin and yang. But until Harry became a Deadhead, his life was filled with much more pain and isolation than it was afterward. We went on tour. We traveled the country together and laughed more than any human being has a right to expect in one lifetime. And when those travels were over, when our little family had all gone our separate ways, Harry tied a rope around a tree and did what he'd been planning on doing all along.

Harry wasn't the only one of my friends who didn't make it back from Dead tour. The rest of us came back physically, but many were pulled down into addictions that they're still struggling with and that will eventually kill them. To be clear, in no way do I equate Grateful Dead music with their problems or with Harry's suicide. My tour brother—Shasta—ended up graduating from Stanford Law School and is now a practicing lawyer in San Francisco (after stints as a percussionist in a touring rock band, a motorcycle racer, bike messenger, and now a tri-athlete). Another one, Sissy, was publicly recognized as one of the most outstanding teachers in the state of Florida. We are biologists, real estate agents, business executives, salesmen, restaurant owners. . . .

If there is a known occupation, there is a Deadhead excelling at it.

In 1988, I did a good portion of the East Coast summer tour in Shasta's (t)rusty green 1977 VW bus. I missed the start of the tour—including shows at the famed Alpine Valley—to attend my high school graduation, then picked up with the band at Buckeye Music Center in Buckeye Lake, Ohio, and on through Pittsburgh, Saratoga, and into Rochester for the hometown show at Silver Stadium on June 30. From there we were off for the July 2–3 shows at Oxford Plains Speedway in Oxford, Maine.

July 2, 1988–Oxford Plains Speedway

> **Set 1:** *Aiko Aiko, Jack Straw, West L.A.
> Fadeaway, Stuck Inside of Mobile, Row
> Jimmy, Blow Away, Victim or the Crime,
> Foolish Heart*
>
> **Set 2:** *Crazy Fingers, Playin' in the Band, Uncle
> John's Band, Terrapin Station, Drums
> Space, The Wheel, Gimme Some Lovin', All
> Along the Watchtower, Morning Dew
> Sugar Magnolia*
>
> **Encore:** *Quinn the Eskimo*

It was Chard, Shasta, and me in the bus on the way out to Maine. Shasta and I had just graduated from high school a couple of weeks before—Chard was actually older than I, but had been held back in seventh grade.

My senior year of high school had pretty much been a joke. I'd spent my spring break on Dead tour, seeing as many shows as I could in a limited span of time (two shows in Hartford, Connecticut; two shows in Worcester, Massachusetts). I hit those shows with Shasta too. He was coming out of the metalhead sector, and I was coming out of the psychedelicized Allen Creek sector, so, in many ways, this early association via the Dead helped break down the often Breakfast Club–like clique system pervasive at Sutherland High School. Shasta and I hit those spring tour shows together in his crappy little 1984 Oldsmobile Omega, nicknamed the Omegadeath Mobile. I still remember him lighting a stick of incense, placing it into a wooden incense holder, and sticking it on the dashboard before we lit up our first joint just after getting onto the I-90 at exit 45. He was a waiflike, elfin creature with a very determined, dominant edge to his personality. I'd put him at 5'7" and 130 pounds at that time. His hair was thin, dirty-blonde, and getting longer. We both wore tie-dyes at that point (eventually our family all but abandoned tie-dye, seeing them as too stock, a little cheesy, something for the locals) and tattered jeans. I mainly wore Chuck Taylor hi-tops, al-

though I'd also purchased the knee-length buckskin
boots with leather laces running up the front that I'd
started working into my wardrobe. My hair had thick-
ened into a substantial brown mini-Afro. Neither one of
us bothered to pack a razor for that trip. I'm quite sure
no one could tell the difference either.

The shows that we saw that spring were outstanding,
but many of my memories of that trip are not fond.
Shasta and I barely knew each other and were far from
the family we would become shortly thereafter. I was
completely enamored of the Dead scene, but was still
clumsy, awkward, and uncertain of how this passion fit
into my larger world. I have always asked too many
questions to fit in easily anywhere. I had found something special with the Dead, I knew that much, but
I was unsure how to assimilate all the new information
and experience into who I was and, more significantly,
who I was becoming. It was frustrating for me to see
more self-assured kids that I knew go to a couple of
shows and suddenly slip into cool Deadhead identities
with the same ease they slipped into girls' pants. If I was
a zealot, I was a problematic one. One who can't just go
blank and absorb the new dogma wholesale. As much as
a majority of people might consider Dead tour something of a La-La Land, when I went on tour I finally felt
like I was in the "real world"; a world of authentic,
sometimes harrowing, often elating experience that was

nothing like the suburban existence I had known up until that point.

Our first night in Hartford, we hooked up with a pack of homeless kids who lived there in the city. They never questioned who I was or where I came from or what business I had stepping foot outside of Pittsford. Shasta and I didn't have any place to crash that first night, and we'd arrived at the site too late, stoned, and excited to get a decent sleeping spot together. These kids weren't Deadheads or hippies. They looked more like skateboard kids do now. I suppose they were sort of scruffy street punks, often called "crusties." I couldn't easily identify them with any group I'd known in Pittsford—and I loved that. Shasta and I ended up roving the streets with these kids as they pointed out some of the places they crashed and told us how they passed their time—getting high, hanging out, spare-changing, messing with people.

I slept that first night in Hartford on a park bench, freshened up the next morning in a public fountain, and by late morning the downtown area was teeming with thousands of people just like me. The fact that the city of Hartford allowed Deadheads to camp out on the lawn of the governor's mansion still makes me chuckle to this day. By showtime, the long expanse of lawn was a Hooverville of multicolored tents, packed bare-heel-to-bare-toe with hippies.

Bob Dylan wrote "Desolation Row," but the Dead often played the song. The lyrics closely paralleled what many Deadheads lived in order the get to a show: skulking around a strange city; high on whatever you could find; hungry, dirty, alienated, free; digging the abandoned streets and feeling your palms sweat every time headlights approach ("the riot squad is restless, they need somewhere to go"). We knew what that song meant. When Bobby Weir sang those words, he was telling you that you weren't alone. And when he sang, "They're selling postcards of the hanging/They're painting the passports brown/The beauty parlor is filled with sailors/The circus is in town" we knew that we brought that too. We were the freaks. The hanged and the ones selling postcards of the hanging. The passports were brown (though, thankfully, the acid was usually not brown, as with the famous Woodstock announcement, "Don't take the brown acid. The brown acid is bad."). The sailors were twirling in skirts. But the peak of that song was always, "The circus is in town." The crowd never failed to respond with a cathartic outburst of approval.

By the time the Maine shows rolled around in July 1988, Shasta and I had closely bonded. With some help from his father (a graduation present), he had traded his old Oldsmobile Omega for the real deal: a 1977 green VW pop-up camper. No more sleeping on park benches

for us! We were out of high school and ready to hit the
road. I had been accepted to Ashland College and
although I was scheduled to start that fall—the whole
idea of going to college was an afterthought at best.
After summer tour, I went to my college orientation
with another Dead family member, Sissy, but didn't
attend any events. We basically just treated orientation
like an amusing stop along tour. He wasn't going to
college and I flat-out didn't care. I vaguely remember
sitting in the back of an auditorium with Sissy during
some sort of presentation about what I should expect
from college life. We snickered like we were watching a
cartoon about life. Sissy went to the rival high school,
Mendon, and we had been out late together at a party in
Pittsford the night before we drove to Ashland. By that
time, the Mendon and Sutherland Dead scenes had
basically merged, which allowed us access to each
other's parties. But the cross-town rivalries were still
percolating, particularly among the jocks (isn't that
who high school rivalries are for?), and at the party
before Sissy and I went to Ashland, a Mendon jock had
squared off with a soccer-playing friend of mine. As
usual, a crowd surrounded the two guys. Their friends
fell into formation behind them. Male aggression
seeded the suburban air like a foreboding storm front.
The party was held in a townhouse in a community
of townhouses across the street from Barker Road

Elementary School. No one was on foreign ground here because we'd all grown up on the same twenty square miles of land. The Mendon jock huffed and stomped and whipped off his shirt. He flexed his pectorals and made aggressive, apelike, combative, territorial gestures. His friends slapped his back to psych him up. My friend basically—and rightfully—made fun of the kid for whipping off his shirt, which only fueled the Mendon kid's aggression further. Things were tight, tense, the crowd was getting hyped, and only a bloody beating would satisfy them. There was only one thing for a stoned-out, peace-loving hippie boy such as myself to do. I walked up to the shirtless, puffed-up Mendon kid and asked him if he thought he was tough. He said that he did. So I kissed him on the cheek and asked, "How tough do you feel now?"

There were two ways that a maneuver like that could go. In one, the kid stares at me for a second and then decides to beat me to a pulp instead of my friend. In the other, the kid folds up from embarrassment or a sudden self-awareness, and the situation is diffused.

Luckily, in this case, my kiss diffused the situation. The kid was stunned. His friends were stunned. My friends were stunned. And then—holy of holies— everyone started laughing and talking about what a fucked-up thing that was to do. The prankster had won out. There would be no fight. But in that small quiet neighborhood, the damage had already been done. The cops had been called, and they rolled up on the assembled gang of kids with their lights flashing. Sissy and I bolted through some yards and watched from the safety of well-manicured bushes as wasted kids were questioned, warned, and told to go home. In Pittsford, that—and a fair amount of authoritative posturing—was usually the extent of police action in breaking up a party. However, one kid's bag of pot was discovered. And Sissy and I watched it all go down. We watched as the cops made the kid upend his bag and dump his pot out all over the lawn. We watched as they gave him a stern verbal warning and sent him on his way. We watched the whole scene closely. Very closely. So closely that when everyone was gone, the party over, and our trip to Ashland about to start, we returned to that exact spot with a flashlight, gathered up the kid's pot from the lawn, and took it with us for the drive up to my college orientation.

I wound up attending Ashland for exactly one semester before dropping out (bitter I had missed so many good shows) and going back on tour.

But before Ashland, there was 1988 summer tour. The maiden voyage for the new VW. Or, as we referred to it, "The Bus." The deeper we got into the Dead, the more our language would reference aspects of Dead culture. Shasta's VW was not a van because a van didn't

carry the Deadhead significance of a bus. In Grateful
Dead history, the Merry Pranksters drove a 1939 American Harvester school bus named Furthur across the
country with Neal Cassady at the steering wheel. As a
result, many Deadheads named their vehicles in honor
of that tradition. A van, or bus, to a Deadhead is as
important and personal as a horse to a cowboy, or a
camel to a Bedouin. Deadheads lived (got to the show)
and died (didn't get to the show) based on their vehicles. They also slept, ate, had sex, conducted business—
lived—in their vehicles. So vehicles were personalized
accordingly. Our family lived in "The Bus." And we
always danced extra hard during "The Other One"
when Bobby spat out: "The bus came by and I got on,
that's when it all began. There was cowboy Neal at the
wheel, the bus to Never-Never land."

Shasta was extremely protective of his new VW.
At least to start with, it was babied, kept clean, spoken
to in soft tones, and loved very much. Cowboy Neal
would not have been allowed to drive. In fact, I was not
allowed to drive. But Chard was allowed to drive.
And here is where Shasta made his first mistake with
the bus.

For me, the standout shows of summer 1988 were at
Oxford Speedway in Maine. The drive to Oxford
Speedway took about nine hours. After about five

hours, Shasta decided he needed a rest. Chard took over driving, and I rode shotgun. We were all wearing shorts, T-shirts, our hair long and shaggy—but after a couple of days at home we were all relatively fresh. It was a beautiful, sunny summer day. We were ready to party. And experiment. Shasta rode along on the green and red plaid couch in the back of the bus. Between the steady roll of the wheels, the slight rocking back and forth, and the engine softly puttering beneath the bed, the couch was a perfect spot for a rolling nap. In fact, it was a challenge to stay awake there. Shasta was soon lulled asleep.

Chard and I drove along the green and rustic northeast listening to bootlegs, speculating about the shows ahead, smoking cigarettes, getting high, and laughing. We were young, free, on the road, and headed for a series of outdoor summer Dead shows with no responsibilities outside of getting to each venue. For obvious reasons (to us anyway), the talk turned to tripping. We both agreed it would be a wonderful experiment to drop acid and drive for hours—for an entire trip even! In fact, this trip seemed like the perfect time to try that out! And as luck would have it, we happened to have some acid on us left over from Silver Stadium.

Predictably, about 45 minutes later we started to "get off" on it. We were having a great time—the sun streamed in the windows; the Maine landscape got denser, greener, more rugged and beautiful—and we giggled at our good fortune. The little VW puttered around narrow curves and slowly worked its way up hills. We giggled harder. We were full-on tripping. We were driving and tripping just as we had speculated about—and it was as fun as we had anticipated.

Until Shasta woke up.

Shasta made his way to the front of the bus, rubbing his eyes, swigging off a bottle of apple juice, and asked where we were. Rich tried to answer, but couldn't form a proper response. His answer amounted to, "Driving. Maine. Outside. Woods." I tried to fill in some blanks, but didn't do much better. Then Chard and I were looking at each other, smirking, trying not to let on that we were completely blasted on acid and clueless about where we were on the trip. "Are you guys?" Shasta looked between us. He was processing the information, starting to understand. "Are you fucking—?" The bus was his brand new baby, and this was its maiden voyage. He had made it very clear that we were to take better care of the vehicle than we would of our own mewling offspring.

The truth hit him solid.

And he was pissed. "Are you guys fucking tripping?!"

To Shasta's credit, he bounced back quickly from this little surprise. Once he ordered Chard to "Pull over! Pull over!" forcing Chard onto a shoulder far too narrow for the wide-body bus, he couldn't help getting caught up in the spirit of the experiment. "I can't believe you guys dosed and drove my van," he laughed, shaking his head out the window.

Better for him to look outside than to risk getting lost in our enormous black pupils.

By the time we neared the Oxford Speedway, traffic was already backed up for several miles down a simple two-lane street. Especially on summer tour, venues tended to be set back on large chunks of land in rural settings, so this sort of traffic jam was not uncommon. In fact, provided you could keep your vehicle from overheating (which basically amounted to turning off the engine), the traffic jam was merely the start of the party. It meant you had arrived. Deadheads flowed freely back and forth between cars—hugs, laughter, dogs, bells, drugs, incense, messages scrawled on cardboard signs, fingers waving in the air for tickets, beads, T-shirts, beer and food for sale. . . . The traffic jam was a temporary extension of the parking-lot scene. And that meant that the marketplace was open for business.

In many ways, the parking lot epitomized a Dead show. Put another way: the parking lot was a Dead show minus the band. The show was there, but the Dead were not. Except they were everywhere. Blaring from enormous speakers mounted on the tops of vans. Trilling out of open car windows past dirty bare feet

hooked around side-view mirrors. Dead tunes leaked
through every tent flap. They danced around every
campsite. The songs were different, but the bootleg
sounds melded together so that walking through the
parking lot was like excavating various Dead musical
eras; the only constants being the core band members
and their surprisingly unchanging hippie constituency.
The smell of the parking lot: patchouli, marijuana, sage,
body odor, grilled cheese, stir-fried vegetables, noxious
sizzling skewers of meat (though those vendors mainly
came out at night) mingling with drug-infused pher-
omones, dirty clothes, mud, dirt, sunshine. . . . An overpowering concatenation of camping smells, sex smells,
hormone smells, hippie smells—the smell of thousands
of people unafraid to cover the natural scents of their
bodies and activities, licit or illicit. The parking lot was
the place to score drugs. Score tickets. Score with cute
little Deadhead chicks and hook-up with kind Deadhead bros. People were ripped off. People were
rewarded for their good karma with free tickets, free
food, or simply connecting with just the right people at
just the right moment. The parking lot was the place to
make connections. Play hacky-sack for hours on end.
Nap in the shade under a rustling blue plastic tarp.
Speculate on the night's set list. Make sure you were set
with doses and a place to crash after the show. Learn a
new song on guitar. Dance to the rhythms of a surpris-

ingly organized and impressively proficient drum circle.
Hear a rant about Wicca. Sign a petition to save the
rainforests. Wander for two hours and still not find the
person, vehicle, or meeting spot you were searching for.

Narcs preyed on the parking lot scene because the
scene was authentic, and it was assumed that we were
all there for a good time. Easy busts abounded. To
avoid detection, every once in a while a call of, "Six up!
Six up!" was passed up and down the rows of the
parking lot, and the Deadheads who made it their
business to know such things knew what this meant:
cops in the area. Keep your drugs out of sight and scoot
to a safer space.

The parking lots of summer shows were the best:
they were usually huge, and often the Dead played for
multiple days. The longer the run of shows, the more
established the parking lot could get. After, say, a three-
day run at Alpine Valley, Wisconsin, you felt like you
had helped establish a new town, put down roots,
learned the terrain, gotten to know your neighbors, and
by the time you left there was a distinct air of sadness
that the community (even if its citizenry was reassem-
bling 48 hours later in a venue two hundred miles
away) would never be quite the same again. City
parking lots were still fun, but you could never shake
the city vibe. The community was still there, still established, but it was less a commune vibe, more a primitive

need to cluster together for strength, survival, and understanding in the face of urban indifference. Many people who went to summer Dead shows will spend their whole story telling you about the parking lot: the bare breasts, the freaks with dreads, the open-air drugs, the peaceful vibe, the raggedy bands of children, the absolutely smiling faces, the patched-together vehicles with license plates from every state in the country and covered, of course, with bumper stickers. Deadheads love bumper stickers. Oh, do they love bumper stickers! They cover their cars, buses, vans with multiple bumper stickers, and they are always on the lookout for the freshest, newest, funniest, timeliest ones. And the parking lot was the place to purchase and check out the best of them: *Bobby Spit On Me. The Fat Man Rocks. Bad Cop No Donut. Not All Who Wander Are Lost. Thank You, Jerry. The Phil Zone. Who Are The Grateful Dead And Why Are They Following Me?* There were official Dead bumper stickers with band logos, characters, and album covers: Steal Your Face, Dancing Bears, Skull and Roses, Blues for Allah, Europe 72, Terrapin Station, Uncle Sam. . . . There were bumper stickers with Jerry Garcia's face from every year and heroic, windblown angle. Particularly on sale in the parking lot, there were unofficial bumper stickers with just about every key lyric (those lyrics that provide the essential "lift-off" moments to songs or that sum up Dead culture the best:

"Let There Be Songs To Fill The Air" "The Music Never Stopped" "Let My Inspiration Flow" "Sunshine Daydream"), along with Dead, hippie, environmentalist, and spiritual mottos, credos, dogma (personal favorite: My Karma Ran Over My Dogma), and general words of wisdom. The parking lot was a fashion show for bumper stickers. It was also a fashion show for fashion. Beautiful handmade dresses, pants, shirts, hats, jewelry, crystals, you name it. Deadheads are masters of velvet and patchwork. Masters of bead and nonprecious stone. Masters of buying cheap clothes in Guatemala and selling them at a substantial markup in the States. And, obviously, masters of cotton T-shirt and colored dye. The parking lot was the center of fashion, food, revelry, and trend.

I didn't have a ticket for the first Maine show. I wasn't worried either. More than any other time in my life, I believed in karma while on tour. I wasn't out to hurt or screw anyone over. I was there for the music, the good times. I was a shaggy young kid on the road with an enormous smile on my face—there were tickets out there waiting to help me fulfill my mission. I had faith in that. And I had the money to pay face value.

We spent the night at a nearby campground filled with Deadheads and got on the road the next morning for the last leg of the trip to Oxford Speedway. Of course, by the time we got near the Speedway, there

was already a huge back-up of cars waiting to enter the
venue. As soon as we hit the traffic jam, I was out the
door of the bus with my index finger waving in the
air: the Deadhead sign that I needed a ticket. I wasn't
stressed out about driving nine hours to a concert I
didn't have a ticket to, and I certainly wasn't going to
let it dampen my spirits. I knew that the lower the
situation brought you, the less chance you had of
scoring what you wanted. I was full of faith in my good
Dead Karma. And, frankly, given the amazing scene
we'd just driven into, there was nothing to feel down
about. At the very least, we'd just arrived at the best
party in the country. As I walked along the string of
cars, people pulled me aside to ask for drugs; to pass
me joints; to try to hand me beers (which I didn't take),
juice, fruit; and to offer advice on who might have
tickets, "A dude just went by here a half-hour ago
selling tickets." But I wasn't about to deal with
scalpers, and they were the ones who tended to be out
actively selling tickets. "Scalper Scum" we called them.
There were even bumper stickers that read, "Die
Scalper Scum," which was as harsh a declaration as
you were likely to see at a Dead show. Scalpers were
making money off the scene in a way that we found
repellent and lechcrous. Deadheads weren't scalpers
and didn't buy tickets from scalpers. I would've rather
missed the show than buy a ticket off a scalper. I wasn't

looking for a "miracle ticket" either. The "miracle
ticket" was a phenomenon unique to Dead shows.
Nobody was shocked to see Deadheads holding up
signs asking for a free ticket. Nor did people who gave
out miracles expect any reciprocation other than a hug
and the knowledge that you had just made somebody's
day. In fact, it wasn't uncommon to hear about richer
Deadheads who bought extra tickets for the sheer joy
of laying a miracle on someone. Of course, Deadheads
love the principles of karma and synchronicity too: you
get what you need when you need it and leave the rest
behind. So while no reciprocity was expected, it also
wouldn't have been surprising to hear about something
groovy happening to the person who gave out the miracle. That was just the way it worked.

But I didn't need a freebie. I had money for my ticket.
Deadheads who needed miracles were common, and
while they weren't looked down on, my tour family
prided itself on being self-sufficient. The scene was
hard enough—we didn't want to be a drag on it anymore
than we needed. And to be honest, we didn't think
much of Deadheads whose survival depended on other
people. There was always a hustle for the enterprising
Deadhead who needed a few bucks. Go figure something out.

We weren't harsh about it. We were just straight-up.

"Hey man, you need a ticket?"

"Yeah," I replied, bouncing happily on the toes of my Converse All Stars. I was dressed in Guatemalan shorts and my favorite Dead T-shirt: a picture of keyboardist Brent Mydland leaning back and to the left while he wails out a solo. It was the only Brent shirt I'd ever seen. While the rest of the band remained stable, the Dead had something of a keyboardist curse. Pigpen was the original Dead keyboardist, but his skills were isolated to the blues. As the Dead got further-out with their sound, Tom Constantine (T. C.) was brought in to add more complex keyboard arrangements to the early Dead albums *Anthem of the Sun* and *Aoxomoxoa*. T. C. toured with the band from 1968–1970 and helped them during a difficult transition time when Pigpen's alcoholism was increasingly debilitating. With T. C. gone and Pigpen in terrible shape, the Dead hired Keith Godchaux to fill the keyboard slot. His wife, Donna Jean Godchaux, also joined the band, becoming the Dead's only female band member. Pigpen died from alcohol-induced internal hemorrhaging shortly after the couple joined the band. Keith and Donna toured for most of the 70s until they finally parted ways with the band in 1979. Keith was replaced by Brent Mydland. Particularly during the late 80s, Brent was bringing more energy to the Dead than anyone else on stage. He was troubled, obviously, but he was also pushing Jerry to new heights and kicking Bobby into spastic vocal contortions that sounded pretty fucking cool at the peak of, say, "Estimated Prophet" or "Let The Good Times Roll." My tour family adored Brent.

"Fifty bucks."

Scalper scum.

"No thanks, man. I don't buy from scalpers."

"There's no tickets around. I just saw someone selling one for seventy-five. You're not going to find one cheaper than fifty."

"Maybe not," I smiled, bouncing and dancing off down traffic jam, "but I don't buy from scalpers." It wasn't an act. Not a bluff. I was as happy as I've ever been and didn't worry for a second that I wouldn't get into the show.

"Hey, brother, come here, come here!" I was waved over to a black limousine. I popped my head in the window. There were a half-dozen men and women partying their asses off inside—not tour Heads, obviously, but not lame assholes either. "Did you just turn down tickets from that scalper?"

"I don't buy from scalpers, man. No way."

"Alright, bro! That's awesome!"

Before I could even agree, I was pulled inside the limousine where I was feted with food and weed. They didn't have a ticket for me, but they loved the fact that I had "shined" the scalper. Good Dead Karma: Do the right thing by the scene, turn down a scalper, and you would be rewarded out of nowhere by rich strangers in limousines. Karma and synchronicity. Twenty minutes later, I climbed out of the limo just a little bit higher than when I'd gotten inside, my pockets stuffed with free pot as a reward for good behavior.

But I still didn't have tickets. And I was reaching the end of the traffic jam. Once the jam opened up into the parking lot, vehicles would fan out in search of the best spots to park and camp for the next three days. In other words, if I didn't get back into the bus by the time it hit the parking lot, I could potentially lose track of them. As with the tickets, though, this wasn't something I worried about tremendously. Even if we got separated—in the era before everyone had a cell phone, mind you—I knew I would be okay.

Good Dead Karma.

Eventually I realized it was time to circle back to the bus to hook up with Chard and Shasta. I hadn't scored a ticket, but I had some new weed to share.

By show time the next day, I still didn't have a ticket. There was no question about what the rest of the family would do: everyone got shut out of a show at some point. Soon enough it was time for them to go inside the speedway, leaving me outside the gates to see what I could pull off at the last minute. I lingered around one of the speedway entry areas with my finger in the air, hoping for that random kind Head who was holding a ticket for someone who never showed up. Inside the speedway, the band started into "Aiko Aiko"—hands down, the best up-beat dance tune opener for an outdoor summer show. Outside the show I bounced. I grinned. I danced. I waved my finger in the air and hopped around in circles, giddy with even the echoes of what was taking place inside. And then I saw it: some Head who'd already gone into the show was poking a full ticket at me through the chain-link fence. The ticket-takers hadn't torn his ticket! Without a word between us, I bolted over, flashed a peace sign (neither one of us wanting to draw any attention to the exchange), snagged the ticket, and zipped back to the left, through the gate and into the show. I was in! "Hey now! Hey now! Aiko, Aiko, un day! Jockomo feeno ah na nay! Jockomo feena nay!" These were nonsense lyrics that meant conditions were perfect for a transcendent few hours of music and celebration. I danced into the speedway, past the seating and down to the floor where thousands of other tripping, sweaty, smiling, blissed-out Deadheads were losing themselves to Jerry's tangy lead line. Without even trying to search for them, I danced through the crowd and straight up to my family who were clustered together and grooving on the floor near the soundboard. We all exchanged hugs, understanding that one of the small and unsurprising miracles that fueled Dead tour had just taken place: Good Dead Karma.

Silver Stadium, June 30, 1988

Set 1: *Box of Rain, Cold Rain and Snow, New Minglewood Blues, Ramble on Rose, Me and My Uncle, Mexicali Blues, Far from Me, Queen Jane Approximately, Don't Ease Me In*

Set 2: *Green Onions > China Cat Sunflower > I Know You Rider, Samson and Delilah, Believe It Or Not, Truckin' > He's Gone > Drums > Space > The Other One > Wharf Rat > Throwin' Stones > Turn On Your Love Light*

Encore: *Brokedown Palace*

Rick was the first one of your group to die. He borrowed his father's new red Corvette to drive to the last day of school in his junior year. In the pictures they published in the newspaper, the front of the Corvette is pushed deep into the front seats. The car was half its usual size, as if a giant hand had reached down, crumpled the car up like old newspaper, and tossed it beside the road. Rick had been "traveling at high speed" when he hit a van, got pushed in front of another car, and then got hit again. Car wreckage was strewn over a 100-foot area. The other driver sustained multiple injuries, including severe facial injuries. Rick survived for an hour while they extracted him from the wreckage. He was pronounced dead at Strong Memorial Hospital at 9:16 A.M.

Your scene outside of school now centers around an apartment shared by anywhere from three to five friends. The inhabitant headcount varies based on who got kicked out of their house that week and who happened to be in town. Some of the tenants have already graduated high school and are just hanging around. For some, this is simply a better alternative than their fucked-up home-life. You all refer to this place as either The Apartment or Alliance Street, where the apartment is located. Alliance Street is the more fitting of the two names. This is the stoner headquarters. The home of the alliance. This is the last gasp of togetherness before post–high school life kicks in and your clique is dispersed to wherever they will go.

This is where cocaine enters the scene and starts to control people's actions in ugly ways. Hash, ecstasy, mushrooms, doses, weed: this is where the standby drugs are too and where you can do them after you score. There is always something shaking on Alliance Street, someone scoring, a card game going on, tunes cranking, a party starting . . . There aren't any girls at Alliance to speak of. The guys with girlfriends don't really want their girls there for any number of smart reasons, including the potential of losing them to one of their friends. Girls can come for parties. But mainly, it is understood that this is a boy's clubhouse.

When Rick dies, there are the calling hours and funeral. You and your friends put on your best clothes and pay your respects to the family. But the real memorial is held at Alliance. Cheap cans of beer are used to toast his hard-partying life. Big joints are passed around with everyone telling stories about Rick and the crazy shit he did. The same shit you all do, really. The bottom line is that you all know that any one of you could have been Rick. Driving too fast. Probably getting high. Definitely jamming loud tunes. You could still be Rick. So you party hard to honor his memory and push back the ghosts.

The Dead are playing Silver Stadium in a few weeks. Everyone at Alliance is going to the show. Rick loved the Dead. The idea comes up to petition the band to play a song to honor his memory. A final, public send-off to your brother. It is a reach, you know, because the Dead haven't played the song in years, but you get together as a group and write a letter asking the band to play "He Was a Friend of Mine." You explain the situation to the band. You tell the Grateful Dead about your friend. What he was like. How he loved their music. How much it would mean to you to have them play the song. You mail the letter and go back to partying, talking about how amazing it would be if they played the song, but really you doubt that the band will ever hear anything about your letter.

But then again . . . they are the Good Ol' Grateful Dead.

Shasta and Tony Silvio drive up to Alpine Valley in the bus in between the end of their classes and the graduation ceremony. You can't make it because you've got finals. They hear about the accident on the radio on their way out of town, but Rick's name isn't given in the report, and Shasta and Tony can't imagine it's anyone they know. Only when they get to Alpine Valley and call home do they learn that it was one of their friends, brothers, in the Corvette that had cracked up and killed that kid on the country road.

The Dead play "He's Gone" at Alpine Valley, and Shasta breaks down in tears.

It's the same at Silver Stadium. The band doesn't play "He Was a Friend of Mine." It's likely they never heard anything about the request. The partying at Alliance before the show is intense, moody, and everyone is

*tripping. This is Rick's show. This is his final send-off. It is
exactly one year after your first show. People peel off and
make their way the short distance from the apartment to
the stadium. The tribe is scattered around the scene with
everyone bumping into each other at intervals before
wandering off to be fascinated by something new and
different. It's summer tour, and the scene is alive and
ecstatic. The band plays "I Know You, Rider" and every
one of Rick's friends at the show feels the chorus "I know
you rider, gonna miss me when I'm gone," beamed
straight to their core. The emotion is building and the
music is hot: you are dancing for the ceremony of it—to
send Rick's spirit a message that he will not be forgotten.
When Phil starts the thick bass line for "He's Gone," it
doesn't matter whether the band got your request or even
if they break out "He Was a Friend of Mine" after all. The
band is "on" for this show. They are tight, the vocals are
crisp, and the music is deep with vibe. Jerry's voice is as
mournful as you've ever heard it. He is wailing your sorrow. He is helping bring all your confusion, anger, and
sadness out into the world where it can be expressed,
purged, and sweated out into the atmosphere. Brent is
topping off the high end of the vocals, and the band down-
shifts into an echoing a cappella chant of "Oh, nothing's
gonna bring him back . . . he's gone, he's gone for
good. . . . Oh, nothing's gonna bring him back . . . he's
gone, he's gone for good." The potential for a bad trip is*

there, but that doesn't happen. Not for you, anyway. This is church. This is home. The music is too honest and soothing. The choice of "He's Gone" seems too meaningful to be a fluke, and besides, you don't believe in flukes. Only karma and synchronicity. It is all coming together. The Dead are singing Rick back home and telling you to keep on going without him. You are young. There is so much to do. He's gone, and nothing's gonna bring him back. Dance, sing, celebrate the life you all still share together. He's gone, children, and nothing's gonna bring him back.

Deadhead Goes
to College
(Briefly)

In fall 1988 I was off to my freshman year at Ashland
College in Ashland, Ohio. Ashland was founded in 1878
as an offshoot of the Brethren movement whose roots
stretch back to the Radical Pietism movement in Ger-
many in the early 1700s. This description of Brethren
dogma comes from the Ashland website: "The Brethren
were characterized by their practice of believer baptism
by trine immersion and their observance of the Lord's
Supper with its three parts: feet washing, love feast and
communion. Their worship services had lively preach-
ing and singing. Their congregations were led by unpaid
or free ministers elected by the local church; they also

had deacons who assisted the ministers and cared for the welfare of the congregation. Brethren people sought to live a devout and Christ-like style of life and to maintain their principles of nonconformity, nonresistance and non-swearing."

Ashland was the strangest place I had ever been.

By the time I arrived there as a freshman, I'd spent a good portion of the summer at Dead shows and the rest of the summer treating Pittsford like a big Dead show. I walked onto that conservative campus a complete freak and immediately stood out like a stripper at a convent. A high percentage of my clothes at that point were multicolored, Guatemalan, made of natural fibers, and completely out of sync with pastel mainstream late-80s fashion. My hair circled my face in a fuzzy, Afro halo. I was tall, thin, and gangly in a way that made every step and movement a disjointed puppet dance that fit well with the constant stream of Grateful Dead songs and lyrics that flowed through my head. I was fluid, I had rhythm, hippie style, but those traits weren't particularly valued in Ashland, Ohio. Some college campuses were very Deadhead friendly in those years— there were strong clusters of Deadheads living together in houses, trading tapes, scoring weed and tickets, etc.— but not at Ashland. I was the only Deadhead at Ashland. And as I walked across the busy quad, I felt like a Rose Bowl float unexpectedly appearing in the middle of morning commute traffic: it was colorful, fun, sure, but what the hell was it doing there?

I was certainly not in college mode either. I was in tour mode. Everything else seemed like a minor distraction. For example: my first day on campus, I skipped the required dormitory orientation meeting in order to buy beer to host a party for everyone on my floor. I figured that I'd have the refreshments ready when the orientation meeting was over—I'd play my part in the orientation process in that way. Unfortunately, I was not present when it was explained that Ashland was a dry campus. Regardless, by the time the meeting was over, the four-person suite I had been assigned to was filled with beer. I began going around the dorm inviting different people I had bumped into that day into the common room between the two-person bedrooms I shared with three other Ohio natives. The party was a great success. People were mingling, laughing, getting to know each other, and since I embraced the role of the freak, the people who took the time to get acquainted seemed interested in who I was and what I was up to. All was well up until, half-drunk, I wandered down to the Resident Assistant's room, offered him a beer, and invited him to the party.

After wiping the astonished look off of his face, the RA escorted me downstairs to where the dorm supervisor lived. I was presented with a piece of paper that was

essentially an admission of wrongdoing on my part.
I was expected to sign this piece of paper saying that
I had done something wrong by having a beer party in
my college dorm, and then I would be punished by the
administration. To me, it was a joke. "No." They didn't
seem to understand what I meant. There was no beer
allowed in the dorm. I had drunkenly offered my RA a
beer on the first day of school. "This paper says that
I did something wrong?" "Yes." "And you want me to
sign it, admitting that I did something wrong?" "Yes."
"No." I shook my Afro, genuinely finding the whole
process amusing. Frankly, I didn't care. If they wanted
to kick me out of college for having beer, then they
could kick me out. I'd just go back on tour. I was there
in my head already. All I needed was an excuse to get
back there physically. "I'm not signing that piece of
paper. I didn't do anything wrong."

We were deadlocked. I didn't see what I had done as
an offense in any reasonable sense of that term. I mean,
who was I offending? No beer at college? When had
that happened? Obviously, I had not done sufficient
research into the school I was attending. With a C
minus average and abysmal SAT scores (it didn't help
that I took them stoned), I'd only gotten into two
schools: Ashland and Wooster College. I don't know if
there is significance that they were both in Ohio, and
I honestly don't know why I ended up at Ashland

instead of Wooster. Again, I barely registered that I was even attending college. And, apparently, the fact that I had missed orientation in order to buy the beer did not help my case with the dorm overlords either. I was the first person "written-up" for a violation at Ashland College that year. Unfortunately, it was not enough to get me kicked out.

I lasted one semester at Ashland College before dropping out to go back on tour. Even after all the places I've been and experiences I've had, I still consider Ashland to be the strangest. The campus was segregated in a way I had only seen in social studies movies about the Civil Rights movement. Although there was no sign posted, there was literally a black section of the cafeteria—not a single white person ate there, and the black students didn't eat in the white section. To a kid raised in Upstate New York, this was astounding. Two black men who were track stars from Cleveland lived across the hall from me. We got high and had some laughs. They had never seen a Deadhead and thought I was pretty far gone, but funny. "Buggin'." Next door to them was a little blond fucker with a scraggly mustache and machine-gun snicker who traced his family back through generations of Ku Klux Klan members and was an unrepentant Klan member himself. He actually had a National Geographic picture of his grandfather at a Klan rally that he proudly displayed on his mini dorm fridge.

Ashland was my first encounter with in-your-face racism (back in Pittsford, it was much more subtle in that urban-suburban, school busing program way), and the experience was akin to bad-trip time traveling. I went to all black parties, where I did my sort of hip-pie-bop dance to people's amusement. I posted Martin Luther King quotes on my door—they were ripped down every week by the Klan asshole and replaced immediately by me without comment. A couple of times, I tried to escape the campus by hitchhiking to Wooster to visit a girl I had briefly dated in high school. There was a small Dead scene there, but the girl had a new boyfriend who wasn't thrilled to have her old boyfriend visiting, so I never stayed long enough to make any connections. One memorable trip, I was picked up by an old man on a motorcycle. I was wearing my green army pants and a beautiful Irish white wool sweater with my multicolored Guatemalan backpack stuffed full of clothes, tobacco, toothbrush, and other supplies. I was high, free, moving down the road and feeling liberated for the first time since I'd arrived at Ashland. The motorcyclist gave me a brown leather helmet and World War II aviator goggles to put on. My Afro popped out the sides of the helmet. I climbed on the back and we rode through the Ohio countryside with me wearing this absurd getup. In the middle of this burst of liberation, the motorcyclist pointed out a long gravel road we were passing with a house visible in the distance that he identified as a high-ranking member of the Ku Klux Klan's house.

However, the capstone weirdness of my time at Ashland was a presidential campaign stop by George H. W. Bush. It still boggles my mind that he would stop at this tiny, out of the way campus in Ohio to give a speech, but I understand a little better now about constituencies and the power of the media to project small venues onto the larger public consciousness. Prior to the visit, a small group of campus Democrats was busy making protest signs. Aside from picking up on some key political issues at Dead shows—I was aware that apartheid, nuclear war, environmental destruction, racism, and the Chinese occupation of Tibet were all very bad—I was basically apolitical. I was tuned in enough, however, to know that Bush was a liar. A former CIA director, how could he not be? But instead of making Democrat signs, I made a sign that reflected my general suspicion of politicians and the American political machine which Bush represented. My sign read:

```
  You Can Try To Close Our Eyes
But We Will Never Turn Our Backs
```

I made my way down to the rally with my sign in hand. The Democrat faction was already out with their signs—marching in a tight little circle, chanting something. The small vocal Republican faction was across from them doing the same. Up until that point, the only outright politics related to the presidential race between Bush and Michael Dukakis that I had noticed on campus were cheaply made, hand-drawn flyers showing a picture of a penis with feet chasing after a vagina with feet. The caption read, "Dukakis, De Bush, it's just one fucking thing after another." I planted myself somewhere between the Democrats and the Republicans and raised my sign. My protest sign was meant to convey a message at a poetic level, not an overtly political level: my own anachronistic Bob Dylan protest statement. I knew the system was corrupt and felt comfortable stating it in a blanket way. I didn't see much need to pick things apart beyond that.

It turns out I was right too. Prior to Bush's arrival, a fleet of buses arrived on the scene, and Bush campaign workers filed out armed with an impressive number of Bush balloons, Bush posters, hats, blowers, and all sorts of assorted Vote For Bush paraphernalia. Within minutes, the majority of the crowd—the ones who showed up without any signs, seemingly there just to hear the speech—were outfitted with Bush gear. Their personalities seemed to morph to fit the swag too. Suddenly the crowd was packed with rabid Bush supporters waving signs and shouting down the little band of Democrats.

At one point, I saw a man with a boy on his shoulders direct the boy to kick down a neighboring Democrat's sign. They were everywhere, chanting for Bush in the middle of nowhere, America. Luckily, the new zealots didn't make much of my sign—was it Democrat? Republican? And while we're at it, what's with that guy? Or was it a girl?—so I found myself relatively anonymous among the partisan jockeying. That's when the media arrived in their own buses. Their timing was impeccable. The Bush people had just turned a relatively tame, vanilla crowd into a raucous Bush rally by disseminating cheap propagandist paraphernalia, and now the media was there to cover the triumphant Bush speech in small-town Ohio. The people there loved him, right? They had turned out in force to support him, right? That's what it looked like on camera anyway. Images from the Bush speech in this shitass little town were projected on news programs all across the country— and, for a moment, Ashland mattered.

To my surprise, a passel of media people dropped their gear in a semicircle around me and my little sign and began snapping pictures. They yelled questions, "What does your sign mean? What are you trying to say?" But, of course, none of them stepped up to ask the questions in a more personal way. And, frankly, I'm not sure what I would have said anyway. I was a prankster. I was messing with the process, the status quo, and voicing my protest against all the dangerous governmental policies that Americans weren't even privy to: the covert, back-door dealings that are widely acknowledged to be the true nature of politics. I was protesting the system, not a specific policy. But the media questioning never got that far. With yet more choreographed precision, George Bush himself showed up on the scene shortly after the media arrived. The entire waltz was stunning. Now the cameras turned to capture Bush, the beloved leader, waving to this vast group of Ohio supporters from the open window of his limousine as he rode toward the field house where he would make his speech. I held a sign that read, "You can try to close our eyes/but we will never turn out backs." Perhaps because the cameras were so close to me, his limo drove close by too. Bush waved to me just like he waved to everyone else in the crowd. Why not? The difference was that when we locked eyes, I flipped him off.

Once I dropped out of Ashland, I was free to tour till my Converse wore out. In spring 1989, I hooked back up with Shasta and Harry, and we hopped into the bus for the entire East Coast tour minus two shows in Milwaukee. We started out the tour with two shows at the Omni in Atlanta, Georgia; then two at Greensboro, North Carolina; two at the Civic Arena in Pittsburgh,

Pennsylvania; two at the Chrysler Arena in Ann Arbor, Michigan; one show at Riverfront Coliseum in Cincinnati, Ohio; one show at Freedom Hall in Louisville, Kentucky; and three shows at Rosemont Horizon in Rosemont, Illinois. I was finally free to do what I had been wanting to do ever since I sat in front of my tape player in 1985, playing and rewinding the song "Ripple" off the Dead's *American Beauty* album over and over and staring at the psychedelic rose on the cover looking for hidden messages in the elaborate lettering and intricately inlaid graphics (and, although I never found it at the time, there actually was one: *American Beauty* can also be read as American Reality). I was following the Dead. I had no commitments outside of getting from show to show. I was on the road, on the bus, on tour, and it was exactly where I wanted to be.

English   Peter Conners
Descriptive essay

The Dead Trip

(1)   Some of the most vivid and memorable experiences
that I have ever had have been at Grateful Dead concerts.
To this day I have seen them fourteen times and traveled
as far as California to do it. I can honestly say that
nothing else that I have experienced has had such a
profound impact on my life. They have opened my mind,
widened my eyes and shown me the true power of music. It
isn't just the concert though, it's the whole enviroment
that you enter at the same time that it enters you.

why shift
to you?
This is a very
personal
perspective,
won't it?
(2)   It all starts with the road trip to the show
which is inevitable as well as being half the fun. It's
not like traveling with your mom and dad to Aunt Bessie's
with the classical music blaring, the dread of your aunt's
sloppy kiss hanging over your head and every other driver
on the road being a "God damned lunatic!" Rather, your   WW
traveling with your friends, listening to your kind of
music and feeling the freedom of the highway. Almost
always on your way to the concert you will see other
Grateful Dead fans, otherwise known as Deadheads, heading   (3)
for the show, especially as you near the city you are
destined for. This gives you a warm, secure feeling inside   cap or not?
READ   because due to caring nature of most deadheads I know that
if I need help they will help me just as I would do the
same for them. The unity that is felt between otherwise
complete strangers, the bond being the Grateful Dead, is
a truly beautiful thing. As you near the stadium you can
read   sense the anxious tension in the car and the excitement
what does this   beginning to grow in anticipation of the good times to
mean? it that   come. Finally you see it, the huge stadium surrounded
do you see?   by hundreds of cars and brightly clad people milling
around. You've made the road trip and the rewards are close
enough to feel. As you find a parking spot and step out
of the car for the first time in hours, you can instantly
hear the cries of deadheads vending their goods. Tie-dye   use death here
T-shirts, braclets, stir fried vegetables, picture's,   see
marijuana and other various hallucinogenic drug's all being   WW
sold right in the parking lot converting it into more of   mul
a carnival than anything else. This carnival atmosphere   (4)
is what attracts many people to start with but it's the
music that keeps them there.

        After a few hours of fun and anticipation in
the parking lot it's time to go into the show. You go
through the gate, walk through the hallway and enter the
main stadium, instantly the smell of marijuana and patchouli
incense smoke fills your nostrils adding to the dreamlike
state you are already in.

SPLICE (two sentences)

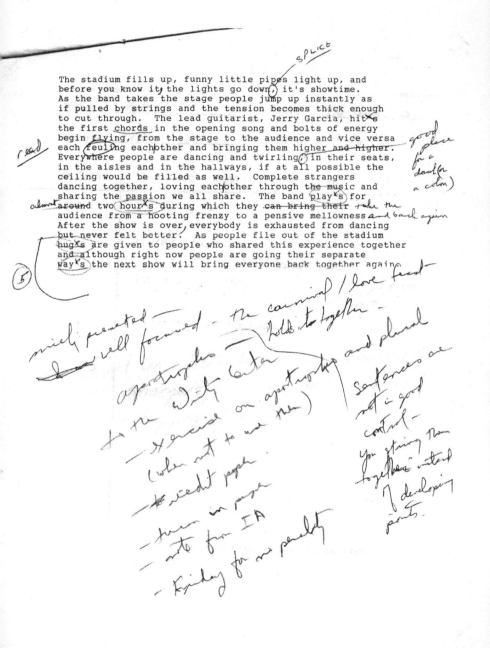

The stadium fills up, funny little pipes light up, and
before you know it, the lights go down, it's showtime.
As the band takes the stage people jump up instantly as
if pulled by strings and the tension becomes thick enough
to cut through. The lead guitarist, Jerry Garcia, hits
the first chords in the opening song and bolts of energy
begin flying, from the stage to the audience and vice versa
each feuling eachother and bringing them higher and higher.
Everywhere people are dancing and twirling, in their seats,
in the aisles and in the hallways, if at all possible the
ceiling would be filled as well. Complete strangers
dancing together, loving eachother through the music and
sharing the passion we all share. The band plays for
around two hours during which they can bring their
audience from a hooting frenzy to a pensive mellowness
After the show is over, everybody is exhausted from dancing
but never felt better. As people file out of the stadium
hugs are given to people who shared this experience together
and although right now people are going their separate
ways the next show will bring everyone back together again

In and Out
of the Garden
He Goes

They encore with "U.S. Blues," so there's no energy bog. "U.S. Blues" is one of the Dead's most straightforward, up-tempo rockers. Most encores ("Black Muddy River" [aka "Black Cruddy River"]; "It's All Over Now, Baby Blue" [aka "It's All Over Now, Grab Your Shoes"]) slow everything down and prepare you for the after-show transition. You gather the possessions you've tossed into the corner during the show—extra clothes, backpack, shoes, etc.—and sway slowly in place as the band winds down. Or else you start winding your way through the hallways toward the best exit, perhaps gathering friends you've misplaced along the way. You are seldom intrepid enough to actually leave the coliseum until the band has absolutely left the stage—even though you know this is the last song and you'd just as soon head out into the night. Why? Because you never know, that's why. And if, God forbid, the Dead busted out some crazy double-encore (acoustic "Ripple," "St. Stephen," Ken Kesey rap) and you missed it to get out to the parking lot, you would—quite literally—never forgive yourself.

But the encore energy flow is different tonight. Tonight they encore with "U.S. Blues." The hallways are electric with dancers spinning, twirling, and jigging. You are not only about to head out into the parking lot, but you're heading to the next show, the next state, traveling down the treacherous thruways of America toward your next encounter with the band. Not everyone will make it. Deadheads will get busted and locked up along the way. Families will get separated. Some might have to leave tour and go back to a job, school, family—that insidious "real world" of America. The Dead know this. They know we're braving the wilds after this, and they know how it is: "red and white, blue suede shoes, you can call this song, the United States blues."

In other words, be safe out there, children. This space only lasts so long and then the authorities close back in. So carry this energy with you back into the parking lot, into the world, down the hallway—whatever you do, don't get busted—and we'll see you at the next stop.

*You're still flying, spinning, grinning, and dancing
when the band leaves the stage. Your family stayed
together tonight. No one split off with other friends.
Everyone stayed together to dance the whole show.
Everyone smoked together during set-break. No one went
on a bum trip. No one was weirded out. Shasta danced
during drums while you and Harry riffed on people walking around the hallways—goofing, playing with reality,
gasping at how easy it is to bend the world into shapes
and how slowly it springs back to its original prefabri-
cated forms. Bart and Sissy are in deep communion on
their trip. Other friends have come and gone throughout
the night, eventually dancing their way down the hallway
into their own personal adventure.*

*But now it's "U.S. Blues": "Back to back, chicken shack,
son of a gun, better change your act!"*

*Jerry nails the "change your act" hard, mimicking
every scolding voice you've heard your entire life, and
putting everybody onto the joke. Here's what you're going
up against. No one here is changing their act. Especially
not Jerry. If anything, we're all in on "the act." Partners
in this victimless crime.*

*You are all together when Bobby mumbles, "Thank you
all, good night." The crowd is wild with excitement from
the rocking closer, and Deadhead eyes are shiny and
bugged-out as they filter out of the coliseum, into the
hallways, toward the glass doors. Once again, Shasta is*

*in the lead. You are behind him, side-by-side with Harry,
both of you still goofing on the world around you as if
matter was a sight gag created solely for your entertain-
ment. Bart has picked up some crusty old Head on the
way out; they are talking slowly and deeply and you do
not want to know what it's about. Sissy is chatting up a
beautiful, young blond girl whose innocence was severely
tweaked—for the better—at the show. He is laughing and
throwing his head back. He is making her happy. As the
Deadhead hordes form a bottleneck at the glass exit doors
the mooing begins: "Moo! Moo! Moo!" People are goofing
on the way we so quickly turn ourselves from dancing
fools into mindless cattle lined up to go back into the
world. Soon the hallways are filled with mooing, and the
sound carries on outside as you pass the exit and are
shuttled down a concrete walkway. You and Harry are
messing with people now. Making other barnyard sounds
to complement the mooing—chickens, a goat, a horse, a
pig—until things get carried away and all sounds work
equally well: monkey, random bird calls, drum sounds,
high chittering laughter. It is weird. Truly weird. And you
are in on the joke and laughing hard as people around you
either get it or don't. It doesn't matter. You are with
family. And you get it.*

*You all stand around the bus while Shasta unlocks it.
For some reason, you expect something miraculous to
happen when the bus door slides open. There is no reason*

*for it. Harry is now with Bart and you and Sissy have,
for some reason, decided that something wonderful—
sparkling gold treasure, or an alien with kind bud—might
have materialized in the bus during the show. You don't
tell anyone else that. Shasta ignores the fact that you're
watching him unlock the door with huge, stupid grins on
your faces. You look at each other and inhale deeply when
the bus door slides open—there is a moment of pure
wonder as you peek inside the bus, first one, then the
other—and then you both fall out laughing and realizing
how fucked up you truly are. You stare at each other,
silent, grinning, and then stand looking at the open
doorway for a few more minutes.*

*"You guys tripping?" says Bart as he blows past and
into the bus.*

"Much?" finishes Harry, joining Bart inside.

*They have picked up veggie burritos along the way.
Bart offers Sissy a bite, which he takes. Then he offers
you a bite, but you can't imagine eating such a thing in
your present state. Food, that is. Completely unneces-
sary—although it would probably be the best thing
for you.*

*You light another smoke instead. You take one last
look around the parking lot as Shasta climbs into the
driver's seat and Bart slams the passenger door. All
around you, Deadheads are making their way back to
their vehicles, their sticker-covered hatchbacks, their*

rusty station wagons, their Frankenstein vans, their family buses. . . . Some look lost in so striking a way that you want to immediately erase their memory from your mind. A tripped out Head stumbles up to you holding out a geode and says "cities" before stumbling down the line. You want to help them. You want them to help themselves. Some are still dancing like the show never ended. Some are looking hard for more doses. Many look as if they've had far too many micrograms of LSD already. People are sweaty; their skin is glistening; their clothes hang off them conforming limply to their bodies, embodying the wrung-out, blissful, exhausted nature of everyone who took the Dead show full tilt. These people or others like them will reappear down the road a couple days from now in Pittsburgh, Ann Arbor, Cincinnati, Louisville. . . . You hope that they find their way there safely.

"Come on, man, hop in, let's get going," Shasta calls out as he guns the puttering little VW engine. Bart has the passenger side window rolled down—his fuzzy arm is resting against the green paint, a woodsy Winston smoking between his fingers. Sissy is sitting on the bed, breaking up weed onto a Frisbee that's resting beside the cluttered sink. Harry is leaning back against the wall with his feet extended toward you. He is staring at you with a grin that says he can see straight through your head and he loves what you are thinking. You are wishing

them peace. You are wishing everyone about to get back on the road as much peace as they can handle.

   "Hey, Space Ranger," Sissy says, looking up at his task, "get in the bus."

   And you do.

CHAPTER
TWELVE

Deal

There were all sorts of ways to make money on Dead
tour. Not all of them were illegal, but the illegal ones
tended to be the most lucrative. Look at it this way: a
sheet of acid consists of 100 individual doses. The
sheets are basically LSD-soaked pieces of stiff paper
with perforations for tearing off individual doses.
Because Deadheads are playful and artistic by nature,
the doses were always decorated with some sort of
design—cartoon figures like Bart Simpson or Daffy
Duck were very popular in the late 80s. There were also
snowflakes, birds, clowns, all sorts of simple images that
could fit onto a surface of about a ¼ inch by ¼ inch.

Interestingly enough, there weren't a lot of doses that replicated official Dead logos. Even while selling drugs, Deadheads were respectful of the band's copyrights.

Depending on your source and the quantity of sheets you were buying, you could get a sheet of acid for anywhere between $30 and $60 in the late 80s. If you had a good relationship with the acid dealer, you could even get the sheets "fronted" to you. In that case, you basically took the sheets for free with the promise that you'd return to pay back the dealer once the doses were sold. Therein lay the pitfalls. The potential for drug deals gone bad. Rip-offs. Opportunistic scumbags. Although I was always a low-level, low-quantity vendor, I did, in fact, get ripped off for an ounce of very good mushrooms that I fronted to a seemingly kind brother named the Mad Hatter at Freedom Hall in Louisville, Kentucky. He was supposed to come back with my money, but never showed. It turned out that he'd played a bunch of Heads the same way—there were a lot of people looking for the Mad Hatter by the end of that tour. Word gets around. I never did see him again, and my guess is that, as Jerry sings in Althea, the "place was getting hot." He either got busted by the cops, or some less passive Heads he'd ripped off caught up with him and taught him a karmic lesson. In all probability, he just scammed a bunch of trusting people and then split tour. Either way, once you start ripping off Deadheads for their drugs, your days on tour are numbered.

Take note, kids: there's no future in being a scammer.

For a real kind brother, though, once you established a relationship with a good supplier, you could support yourself on the road even if you started with nothing. Provided you didn't get busted.

Doing some basic math (the only kind I'm capable of), you can quickly figure out the economics of selling acid on tour. Let's say a sheet costs $50. In a standard parking lot transaction, you'd sell one hit for $5 or three for $10. Even selling single doses, it only takes 10 hits to pay for the sheet. That leaves 90 more doses of pure profit. Staying with our one hit per customer scenario—minus 10 hits for you and your friends—that's a profit of $400 on a sheet of acid. One basic day on tour, you might spend $20 on a concert ticket, and, even if you were "styling" (eating well, smoking good weed, etc.), you'd still only be talking another $25–$30 per day for expenses (depending on gas, where you were with your pot supply, and so forth). So let's round our daily expenditure number to $50 a day (again, much higher than I lived on), and round our days per week off too.

In the end, by selling one sheet of acid you could realistically style on tour for a solid week.

Now, I did do other things to support myself on tour. In fact, I even (gasp) worked at straight jobs before tour started so that I had money in my pocket when the bus pulled out of town. But I was just about the crappiest employee you could imagine. Flat out, I just didn't give a fuck. I didn't care about keeping the job, and I didn't give a damn about the people I worked for. This shitty work ethic had two main roots. One, the jobs were respectable, but in my mind they sucked. I worked as a busboy, a grocery store bulk food employee, a garden center employee, a grunt house painter . . . I hauled around cylindrical tubes of meat in a disgusting meat packing plant . . . I put together shelving . . . I put on a nice shirt and made photocopies in a cubicle for eight hours a day . . . I sealed envelopes for a health club promotional campaign . . . I even had a job picking up plastic bags and newspaper that had blown off the top of a landfill and gotten stuck on the surrounding fence. My coworkers were entirely Laotian immigrants, and even though we couldn't communicate, it was obvious that they wondered what the hell I was doing there. They looked at me during lunch and then said things and laughed to each other with big, wide smiles. I smiled back uneasily. They ate fish and vegetables for lunch. I had some sort of sandwich I was afraid to pick up for fear of what was now on my hands. That landfill should have been closed years before I got there. It was completely overstuffed and smelled exactly as you'd expect an expired landfill to smell. As Thomas Hobbes would observe: it was a nasty, brutish business.

As should be obvious, the other reason for my poor work ethic was that these jobs were completely divorced from my reality at that point. They were just as divorced from my true concerns as school was. That wasn't where I wanted to be. It was where I had to be to get to where I wanted to go. My only interest was in surpassing these straight obligations to get back on the road. So sometimes, I sucked it up and did what I needed to do to get enough money to launch me back on tour. Then once on tour, the money came easier, but at much higher risk.

And how, a citizen might ask, did you manage to sell, say, 80 hits of acid to strangers at a concert in a city you'd never previously set foot in?

This is a good and reasonable question.

The answer is—it wasn't a concert. It was a Dead show!

Freaked out kids walking around muttering "Doses, doses" was par for the course. You might also hear "Doses, X, Shrooms" or "Doses, X, Shrooms, Kind Bud," and so on. Basically, whatever the person muttered, that's what they were selling. It wasn't as if I was the only one doing it. People expected to be able to come to a Dead show and pick up the drugs they were looking for. No one looked at you askance for selling drugs at a Dead show. You were actually providing a valuable service. In fact, you were risking your own security to provide this valuable service.

And there were plenty of idiots selling drugs who could keep the cops busy. Brain-fried Heads who would advertise too loudly and sell to anyone who came into their line of vision. That wasn't me. I took a good, hard look at the person before I ever let them know what I was selling. If their tie-dye looked too crispy, just out of the box; if they were more than five years older than me; pretty much, if they were wearing a bandana on their head of any kind—I didn't sell to them. I just kept walking. I kept my ears open for the call "Six Up" that meant cops were in the vicinity. And, if need be, I could easily give up eating a meal if it meant avoiding a sketchy deal.

Plus, once you had your connections, you didn't have to limit your sales of weed and psychedelics to when you were on tour. In the early 90s, I was going to shows while I was enrolled in college, so I had a healthy market of collegiate peers. That was as easy as dealing got. Plus, again, I was providing a valuable service. With Deadhead and stoner friends riddled all over the East Coast colleges, it was never a stretch to buy and sell shit when you needed a little bump of cash for the next tour without having to get a regular job.

In the ultimate bonus plan, this extended to my visits to my girlfriend's college.

I wouldn't say that I brought all the drugs to my girlfriend's college. They certainly had plenty of their own.

But—particularly in the first couple of years, freshman
and sophomore for her—I seldom arrived on campus
empty-handed. My high school girlfriend had ended up
at a small, liberal arts college called Allegheny in
Meadville, Pennsylvania. As it turns out, she was one of
five people from my graduating class who decided to go
to Allegheny. That wasn't too surprising—people from
our high school had consistently gone on to attend that
school. We also knew people from neighboring schools,
including Mendon, who started the same year as my
girlfriend. Allegheny was—and is—an exceedingly
pleasant little campus nestled in the sleepy bosom of an
otherwise nonexistent Pennsylvania town that, without
the school, would exist only as a piss-stop exit on your
way to Pittsburgh. Girls roamed to class in the early
hours wearing pajama bottoms and sorority sweat-
shirts. The boys were not the best athletes in their high
schools—not the most popular nor most attractive—but
they were certainly high on the totem pole. At Allegheny, the future successful ones mingle, fall off into
drunken trysts, and wake up guiltless in the morning.
Why should they feel guilty? They were doing exactly
what they were supposed to be doing. Being typical,
natural college students.

My Allegheny girlfriend didn't do drugs. This was
one of the pleasant holdovers from high school society.
She and I had become best friends and lovers beyond
the landscape of adult (or collegiate, semi-adult)

mores. We had first dated when we were fifteen years old. My girlfriend was always smart, social, and supported by a warm and involved family. At fifteen, I was staring down the barrel of the dissolution of my family unit. Dale Davis, one of the country's foremost writers/educators specializing in at-risk youths, believes that children of divorce were particularly attracted to the Grateful Dead. She believes that Jerry served as a paternal figure for kids who had lost the daily presence of their fathers. Because mothers are more likely to retain parental custody of children, there is an archetypal truth and logic to this observation. I can certainly testify that many—if not most—of my fellow travelers came from homes broken by divorce or death. Coupled with the re-creation of the family unit, this observation sees Deadhead children of divorce conjuring a makeshift nuclear family unit when their own families are wrenched apart and away from their control.

My parents were not divorced. Nevertheless, in my early teens, the makeup of my family changed drastically. I am the youngest of four children. My next closest sibling—my only sister—is six years older than me. While growing up, I was surrounded by siblings who fawned over me and treated me like an omnipresent mascot. I danced for them. Sang. Cheered them on from the sidelines of their sporting events. I hid beneath their

beds, eavesdropped on their phone calls, and learned a
great deal about being a teenager before I ever reached
double-digits.

But by the time I turned thirteen, my house was
empty. My siblings had gone on to college and, in the
case of my oldest brother, graduate school. My father
had advanced in his career at Kodak to the point where
he had an office in Washington, D.C., where he spent
much of his time. As I mentioned, I knew how to be a
teenager—including the all-important rebelling against
authority—before I ever reached my teen years. My
mother didn't have a prayer of controlling me. I was
pissed at being left alone and had been waiting years to
party, drink, smoke, and hook up with girls. I had
watched this all go on—and I liked it. I wanted it.

And that's what I did.

By the time I started dating my girlfriend at fifteen,
I was already walking a rebellious strut. I wasn't partying as heavily as I would by the following summer, but
I was on the road. My girlfriend—a sweet, successful,
pretty suburban girl—was attracted to this rebellious
attitude. The classic good girl/bad boy scenario. But I
still had short hair. Nice manners. And, most importantly, sensitivity. I was already writing poetry. I could
verbalize my ideas and perspectives, and I knew how to
talk to girls. I was a good kid, but on the brink of problematic drug use and complete "fuck-you" rebellion.

So my girlfriend and I got to know each other before my complete fuck-you phase kicked in. We connected over our mutual sensitivity and need to express ourselves. We recognized each other before social pressures could drive us apart.

Did I mention that I married this girl? That we now have three children of our own? That she is still my love and best friend?

Our story toward marriage wasn't without its villains, plot twists, and melancholy Sundays. We were apart. We were together. We were apart. But in the end, we were together.

And did I mention that Jay from Pittsford went to Allegheny College too?

That really helped my drug sales on campus. Normally, I would arrive on campus and go straight to my girlfriend's dorm or apartment. Soon after, the phone would ring or there would be a knock at the door. Jay. Jay and a posse of his friends. They would be jumping around, slapping me on the back, ready to rage and party. With little or no chance for my girlfriend to protest, I was pulled out the door and into wherever the gang was regularly partying that month. Someone's dorm room or off-campus apartment (we were still too young to get into bars).

When I hit Allegheny, I almost always had something interesting with me. A quarter pound of good, green bud. A sheet of acid. Mushrooms. Ecstasy.

The basic Deadhead staples.

And if I didn't have these things, well, these guys usually had some of their own.

We would party, laugh, listen to tunes, and bond, and a couple of hours later my girlfriend would show up. She'd give me a cute, shaming nod of her head. This wasn't her scene. But I knew she didn't mind too much. She knew I was partying, but she didn't know I was selling drugs. It's not something we ever discussed. She loved me beyond that shit. Or perhaps in spite of it. And I loved her even though she didn't party.

So the economics of selling drugs to support my touring habit made sense. At the time, they were certainly more appealing than working straight jobs to pay for an entire tour. Knowing how money works on the road, that may have been impossible anyway. If I had the money, I would've spent it fast and early. Being forced to make money as you go also slows your spending and forces you to live, as the recovering addicts say, one day at a time.

I did sell legal things on tour too. Usually, my tour family would pool together our money to sell these legal products. You could buy a few 12-packs of Mountain Dew at a grocery store and sell them for $1 apiece. You could do the same thing with Bass Ale—a popular stylin' brew on tour at that time for some reason—but the fact that we were underage for a lot of tours made that a trickier proposition. A lot of Deadheads made very good food—there is actually a book called *Cooking with the Dead* by Ellen Zipern that compiles Deadhead recipes from show parking lots and couples them with profiles of the Deadheads who she got them from. And that was the problem—there were too many people selling very good, healthy, and organic plates of food or "fatty burritos" on tour. None of us could cook anything fancier than a grilled cheese sandwich. So we sometimes sold those. But not often. The same goes for clothes and jewelry. There were just too many skilled Deadhead artisans and clothing traders on the scene to try to compete. One tour, I did venture into crafts vending to mixed success. I knew a guy from my high school who had gotten into making juggling sticks. These consisted of two small dowels—about 2 feet long, ½ inch in diameter—and one larger dowel—about 3 feet long, 1 inch in diameter on each end. The larger dowel was shaped on a lathe to create an hourglass design. When lathed correctly, you could place your finger in the middle of the larger stick and it would balance with ease. These sticks were then wrapped with different colored, fitted strips of leather that were glued onto the wood.

This guy from my high school lathed the wood for me and schooled me in how to make the juggling sticks. I left for West Coast spring '89 tour with all the makings for about twenty pairs of them. Perhaps the best thing about the whole endeavor was that it was a great way to pass time on the road. I was cutting, fitting, and gluing pieces of leather all the way across the country. At rest areas, I practiced juggling with them because that was how you attracted buyers. You had to show them what your sticks could do. I got pretty good with them— twirling the big stick on one of the smaller ones, then flipping it into the air and catching it with the other two sticks and seamlessly continuing juggling. I was good, but again, there were serious craftspeople making these things and Deadheads so skilled at playing with them, they could've landed off-tour gigs with Barnum & Bailey.

I made, sold, and played with the sticks through the whole West Coast tour. I don't remember exactly, but I seem to remember selling them for $20–$25 each. So while they did bring in some money, they were more fun than lucrative.

Interestingly enough, those sticks also gave me the only crisis of conscience I ever had while selling stuff on tour. The sticks were colorful and looked like fun. So, of course, Deadheads, and especially children, were attracted to them. I remember standing in the parking lot of Autzen Stadium in Eugene, Oregon. It was the end of summer tour. I was down to my last pair of sticks. Over to my right, Ken Kesey was sitting atop a shiny, cleaned-up, updated and roped-off version of the Furthur bus surrounded by onlookers. I'd been on the road for a long time, and scenes like that had ceased

to faze me much anymore. Still, I knew enough to sell
the sticks near the bus. That's where the crowd was.

I was juggling the sticks, dancing around, content,
hirsute, and stoned. I looked down and there was a
kid—maybe eight years old—standing in front of me. He
was a cute little boy, but it was obvious he'd been on
the road most of his life. His clothes were dirty, and he
looked underfed. One thing that often goes untold in
the Deadhead story is the fact that there were kids who
grew up on tour. They sometimes roamed in Dickensian
packs around the parking lots. Their hair was long,
unwashed, and they had a wary, hardened look well
beyond their years. I suppose it could be claimed that
these kids were "home-schooled," but I sincerely doubt
anything close to education was touching their young
minds. And there were a lot of creeps on tour their
parents should've been afraid they'd encounter. Drug-
fried motherfuckers who you wouldn't want looking at
your kid, much less interacting with them.

I looked down at this little boy and immediately
made him for a tour kid. He came up to me on his own,
no parents in sight, and stood watching me juggle the
sticks. He had on a ratty T-shirt, dirty shorts, long
twisted hair, and a deeply suntanned face. I stopped and
handed him the sticks so he could give them a try. I sat
down on the dusty ground next to him and tried to
show him how to juggle; how to wedge the middle stick

between the smaller dowels, toss it up into the air, and start knocking it back and forth in the basic juggling method. We were having a good time. I liked the kid a lot. After all this time, I still do when I think of him. The kid told me he had been looking for me for a long time. He'd seen the sticks at some show along the way, and he'd been wanting a pair. He didn't want the other kinds—the kinds that were no doubt better made, but obviously not as cool looking to his little eyes. He wanted my sticks. My heart was breaking. This was the end of tour, and I needed money to kick in for gas and tolls back to the East Coast. This was my last pair of sticks. And this kid wanted them. And that meant he'd have to have the money.

Finally, his dad came over to us. Perhaps he had been watching us all along. I liked the way he looked. He carried himself a little uneasily and made no show of having everything he needed. He seemed like a good man. Certainly a good Deadhead. Trying to be a good father. You could see it in the way he carried himself and the way he talked to the kid—as an adult, yes, but with paternal compassion. He didn't look like he had any money. He looked like he was living hand-to-mouth with his family on tour.

The boy asked his father for the money to buy the juggling sticks. Just like any kid who wants something— he put on a show, saying how these were the ones he "really wanted" and that he'd been looking for. The father nodded, shuffled his feet. He didn't put up much of a fight. Perhaps he'd already promised the kid the sticks whenever he found them. Perhaps he figured the kid would never actually find them.

But the kid did find them.

Before the father could rustle through his Guatemalan fanny pack for the money, I handed the kid the sticks and waved away any money. How could I take it from them? Ken Kesey was waving to the crowd. The crowd was pressing in against the rope that kept them away from Furthur. This was Eugene, Oregon. The show was going to start soon. West Coast tour was almost over.

Madstop

My biological family is very educated and accomplished.
My three siblings, by birth order, are a doctor (who also
holds two master's degrees), a dentist entrepreneur, and
an MBA who owns her own business. My father has a
PhD in mechanical engineering, and my mother's side of
the family is filled with doctors and professionals with
advanced degrees. Although I never clicked with formal
education, it never crossed my mind that I would blow
off college completely. Ashland had been a bust. It was
the exact wrong place for me. As a result, I had been able
to tour solidly through spring and summer of 1989 with
minimal interruption. But I always knew that I would

have to go back to college eventually. So while I was home between shows—and while my sister stood over me, visiting home from her apartment across town where she was living while getting her MBA—I fired off a few applications to SUNY schools. It seemed like the most logical decision at the time. State schools gave easy geographic access to East Coast tour and to most of my friends. Getting into one would keep my parents and family off my back. Plus, they didn't cost very much, so I wouldn't feel too guilty that my parents were dumping tens-of-thousands of dollars into my tuition for classes that—when I bothered to show up—I was too stoned to comprehend.

Despite my poor academic record and abhorrent standardized test scores, I was accepted into SUNY Potsdam College for the fall 1989 semester.

I arrived on campus with an ounce of weed to sell and all my belongings packed into a couple of bags. Once again, Sissy had driven me off to my college experience. We brought my things up to my dorm room, smoked a bowl, and then he drove off back to Rochester and his job delivering pizzas. Unlike me, Sissy always had an outstanding work ethic. He kept that job delivering pizzas for close to ten years.

At Potsdam, I was housed in a suite in the top floor of the tallest dormitory on campus: Bowman. The suite consisted of a small entry room and a larger second room with enormous windows looking out over a vast green field that led to the field house. Despite the drab, white concrete walls, it was actually a pretty cool room.

Potsdam is home to two colleges—SUNY Potsdam and the private school, Clarkson University. Fifteen minutes up the road is another highly regarded private school that my father had attended on scholarship, St. Lawrence University. The Raquette River runs through the town of Potsdam, adding a peaceful, meandering feel to the sleepy town. Ever since the 1950s and 60s, Potsdam has also been fertile musical territory. Back then blues players needing gigs between Canada and larger, better-paying cities like New York, Chicago, Philly, and St. Louis would stop and play a one-off gig at a local bar. Usually either the Down Under or Maxfields. As years went by, the small town's reputation as fringe, musical, and perhaps a bit wacky was further solidified as hippies moved to the North Country in large numbers while the 70s closed in fast and hard all around the country. These recent long-haired transplants bought cheap land; grew vegetables and marijuana; opened food co-ops; spent four months of solid winter playing acoustic instruments in front of wood-burning stoves; and raised their children on granola, fresh milk, and bartered venison.

My first roommate at Potsdam was a cocky white basketball recruit with a shaved head and large collection of bad rap CDs. He informed me on our first day that he would not be staying there and, true to his word, moved out within a week to join four other basketball players in a five-person suite in nearby Lehman dormitory. Following the move, he ignored me when we passed on campus. He was a jock. I was a hippie.

After that roommate, I was assigned Mike, a psychotic North Country native with a heavy metal CD collection and a large array of small and deadly weapons—hunting knives, switchblades, brass knuckles, throwing stars—which were his pride and joy. Mike had been thrown out of his first dormitory for pulling an air rifle handgun on a first-year girl coming out of the hall bathroom. Apparently she'd shrieked loud enough to get the Resident Assistant out of her room; the terrified teenage girl then ran inside the open door, pushed the RA in, and slammed the door behind them. By the time the RA had convinced the girl that it was safe to check outside, Mike was doubled over in laughter beside the drinking fountain in the hallway. It was a joke, he insisted then and always, and the administration must've agreed because rather than suspend Mike or kick him out altogether, they simply allowed him to move in with me. Nowadays, post-Columbine, I doubt the school would be so kind. So for three weeks, while Mike and I lived together, I was awakened every morning to the dream-shattering power chords and bloodthirsty vocals of Dokken, Megadeath, and early Metallica.

Every morning, psychotically loud, at 8:00 A.M.

Luckily Mike had also informed me, right from the start, that he didn't intend to live with me long. A buddy of his from Dungeons and Dragons club was looking to change rooms, and they were going to try for a double together. Three weeks later they got it, and Mike moved out. He also ignored me on campus after that.

Fortunately, I had made a new friend my first day at Potsdam. I'd been walking across campus to get cigarettes in town when I passed a kid with long, curly black hair and a tie-dye. Although we'd never met, the tie-dye and our general laid-back demeanors gave us an instant connection. Instead of the usual "wassup?" nod in passing, we stopped. We started talking. Instantly, a new friendship was born. Douglas was from a suburb of Albany, and our backgrounds were similar enough that we could've grown up together. Plus, he was cool as hell. Once we started talking about the Dead, the connection was set. Not only did Douglas go to shows and love the band, but he was a musician. He could actually play the music. Douglas was primarily a drummer, but at that time he could pass on guitar and had taken years of piano lessons too.

We separated with the agreement that I'd meet him back in his dorm room after I went into town. Sure enough, when I got to Douglas's room a couple of hours later, he was in there playing a classical guitar. He had an enormous, beautiful, tie-dye tapestry hanging over his cheap little dorm bed. Douglas hadn't spent too much time mastering the instrument, but at that point I was impressed by anyone who could bang between an A major and an E major to play "Aiko Aiko." I mentioned in passing that I'd always wanted to play guitar and, without another word, Douglas handed me the classical guitar. He showed me a couple of chords and told me to take it back to my room. He wasn't giving it to me. But—knowing me for only an hour—he was loaning it to me indefinitely. I wanted to learn guitar, so he gave me his.

By the time Mike moved out of my dorm room, we had arranged for Douglas to move in. The bad rap and heavy metal CDs moved out, and more Dead bootlegs and Douglas's instruments moved in. The first thing we did when Douglas moved in was to rearrange the room. First we dragged our mattresses off of the rickety metal bed frames and arranged them in the small entry area. The entry area was just large enough for the two mattresses, a television set, and a nightstand to put between us—so that became our new bedroom. Next we hung Douglas's large tie-dye tapestry beside the mattresses to create the illusion of a hallway running from the front door to the back room, separating off the tiny bedroom area. After that we covered our empty bed frames in the main room with blankets and pillows, turning them into uncomfortable sofas, and placed a couple of trunks in the center of the back room to act as coffee tables. Once we added Douglas's stereo, his guitar, his drums and percussion equipment, a red light, our combined tapes and CDs, various band posters, and my little blue bong, we had built what became known as The Jam Room.

From that point on, I no longer just listened to music. In fact, I would never listen to music the same way again. I was completely absorbed by the guitar. On one trip back home, I had dragged my brother's old acoustic out of his closet and made it my own. Douglas and I played music at every spare moment. He showed me chords, and because he wasn't allowed to play his drum kit in the dorm, guitar became his main instrument for that year too. We played all the Dead tunes and covers we could pull off: "I Know You Rider," "Eyes of the World," "Franklin's Tower," "Bertha," "Going Down the Road Feeling Bad," you name it. Not only was I playing, but Douglas was encouraging me to sing as well. Suddenly, I was doing it! I was making music! As a result, the Dead were being broken into their composite parts to an extent that they never had before. I had never played an instrument, so I hadn't been able to isolate the techniques that went into making the music. I had observed musical interplay ever since watching Jay's band back in Pittsford, but I had never experienced it myself.

Most important, though, Douglas and I were writing songs together. I'd always carried my notebook of poems and nursed along my fledgling metaphors and images. Now we were setting them to music! Suddenly, the lyrics of Robert Hunter and John Barlow took on more meaning to me as well. I was barely squeaking through my classes, but I was staying up late into the night trying to match word with music, and grasping the challenges and joys of the writing process as I never had before.

In one year, I had gone from music fan to fledgling musician and lyricist. As with all new artists, my passion for the process eclipsed my facility, but that didn't matter either. The important thing was that I was doing it. I was making music.

Sophomore year, Douglas and I moved in together in a shabby three-bedroom house off campus. We took our little Jam Room scene and expanded it to fill our new house at 110 Main. Our third roommate was a Clarkson dropout named Tom. Tom had come to the United States from Australia on a student visa that was no longer valid. In other words, he was an illegal immigrant. Tom had dreadlocks down to his waist. He never wore shoes and showered, at most, once a week. He didn't like the Grateful Dead. He liked prog rock. He also loved chemistry, pot, stray dogs, and—above all—Carlos Castaneda books. It seems so naïve to me now, but Tom was the first friend I had who was, by all outward appearances, a hippie but not a Deadhead. As an adult who looks basically straight, but remains a Deadhead, I now understand that Deadhead and hippie are not synonymous terms. Hippies can be Deadheads. Deadheads can be hippies. But the two labels are, in reality, mutually exclusive. However, up to that point I had never met a hippie who wasn't a Deadhead. I didn't even know it was an option.

Tom wasn't the only non-Deadhead hippie at Potsdam either. In fact, most of the friends I made in college were hippies—or, at least, hippie-sympathetic—who weren't Deadheads. Many were born and raised in the North Country where long hair, T-shirts with flannels tossed over them, sandals or shitty sneakers, and pot smoking were simply a given. They didn't mind the Grateful Dead. They just didn't care much one way or another. They were just as likely to love Rush as Bob Dylan.

The scene up in Potsdam was very accepting. With all the colleges clustered in the area, the Greek system was strong and very present. Amazingly, though, our hippie scene, though much smaller, had an even stronger impact on the life of the campus. There were a lot of freaks up there in the North Country. And, almost immediately, the freaks found each other and formed our own social scene. And we were an industrious bunch as well. There were hippie freaks writing for the school newspaper. Hippies organizing recycling campaigns and major Earth Day celebrations. Hippies acting in school plays. Hippies giving dance recitals. Hippies wearing bowlers, ponchos, and long beards, waving to each other across the crowded quad between classes. Hippies raising their hands and asking socially and environmentally conscious questions in class. Hippies getting stoned with political science and philosophy professors at off-campus parties.

At one point, the National Security Agency (NSA) made the mistake of publicizing a recruiting visit to Potsdam's campus. We were having none of it. Although they saw the protest coming and tried to keep us out by switching rooms and meeting times, we had inside sources who kept us informed. Remember: there were hippies everywhere. A little freak NSA of our own. We crashed the NSA's information meeting and took every available seat not occupied by earnest, straight-laced students contemplating a career in citizen surveillance. We lined the walls; stared the agents down; and asked questions that were probing, rude, absurd, and generally disruptive. And when the NSA agents quickly packed up and got into their cars to leave, we literally chased them out of town on our bicycles, yelling at them and applauding each other like we'd just won the war. Or at least a small battle.

There were also many talented musicians around Potsdam. And many hippies who appreciated live music. As a result, our jam room at 110 Main became ground zero for almost-daily jams with anyone who wanted to play music taking part. Don't play an instrument? No problem, here's a cowbell. Make a joyous noise. Douglas's drum kit was always set up, and there were always at least a couple of guitars plugged in and ready to rock. It wasn't at all uncommon for me to come home to find the jam room cooking with great live music and neither Tim, Douglas, nor I even there. The door was always open. People dropped in anytime they wanted and everything—food, beer, weed, hallucinogens, you name it—were shared communally.

The final resident of our house was a hardcore North Country biker named Randy. Just as the Potsdam crew were the first non-Deadhead hippies I met, Randy was the first hardcore biker I knew. His Harley was his life. That motorcycle and the black leather boots on his feet and leather jacket on his back were, literally, his only possessions. Randy was in his mid-forties and basically came as a package deal with Tom. They had both been in Potsdam for years and were the most noticeable outsiders in the town. In some ways, they were an incongruous twosome: the biker and the dreadlocked hippie. However, knowing my hippie history, this part actually made sense to me. The Hell's Angels had played a prominent—if not always positive—role in the first hippie scene in San Francisco back in the 60s. They continued to be an omnipresent part of the scene right up until the end. But neither Tom nor Randy had any knowledge or interest in that history. They were just outsiders who both loved pot and enjoyed each other's peculiar company. They both grew amazing weed and were under constant surveillance by the local police too. As a result, Randy lived with us in fall and spring (in winter, he "twisted the wick" on his Harley and rode out to Texas to work in the oil fields), and 110 Main became a fixture on the patrol route of local cops looking to make their presence known. Randy paid his rent by leaving big buds of killer outdoor grown pot around the house for us to find. Take a piss, spot a huge kola bud on top of the toilet. Open the fridge, find a stinky nugget on top of the margarine container. Douglas made money playing music at gigs and as a percussionist for the dance department. Tom worked as a lab assistant at Clarkson. I sold weed to make side money while my parents paid the rent (about $100 per month). All was well in the North Country that year.

CHAPTER FOURTEEN

Now Let's Go
Run and See

The following flyer was circulated at Richfield Coliseum on September 9, 1990. It contained the below letter on one side and the lyrics to "Ripple" on the other. No author was attributed.

Ripple at Richfield Coliseum 9/9/90
A Tribute to Brent Mydland and The Grateful Dead

As most of you know, this is the first Grateful Dead concert since the death of keyboard player Brent Mydland on July 26. To remember Brent, and to celebrate the continued life of the Grateful Dead, we would like you to lend your voice in a crowd rendition of "Ripple" at the beginning of the 2nd set.

The signal to start will be when Bob walks on stage after the Intermission. If you are close enough to see this, hold a match or lighter in the air to alert others in the Coliseum who may not be able to see as clearly. There should also be several helium balloons released at this time. The lyrics to the song are on the back of this sheet. Sing it straight through, keeping the pauses between the lines, but not the instrumental breaks between verses.

The idea to sing "Ripple" at this start of a new era was suggested by Dead Heads on the West Coast, who had planned to do it at the now cancelled Shoreline concerts that were to occur last weekend. This leaves the ball in our hands. This particular song was chosen for many reasons. It is widely known, it has a simple melody, and most importantly: its lyrics carry a message of both longing for the past and hope for the future.

Many people have put their time and effort into getting this sheet in your hands. We hope that you will lend your part in this tribute so that 20,000 songs will fill the air. If you see a neighbor without one of these handouts, please share yours with them so that they can sing as well.

This will work, and work well, if everyone stays alert at the start and lends their voice. Try to do your part, we need a silver lining to the dark clouds of recent events!

♻ this flyer is printed on recycled paper

Please Don't Litter and we hope you Enjoy the Show!

By the time I discovered the Beat writers during my
junior year at SUNY Potsdam I was already well primed
to embrace their writing and ethos. Through Douglas's
patient teaching and generous spirit, I had picked up
enough guitar to begin playing in bands and performing
my own songs in front of audiences by junior year.
Douglas had transferred to the Naropa Institute (now
Naropa University) in Boulder, Colorado, by then to
pursue a music degree. Before joining my own band,
I had spent weekends working the sound board and
being a roadie for his college band, Fathead Minnow.
After he left, I started playing with members of Fathead
Minnow and some new guys in a band called Artie
Wigglefoot and the Traveling Medicine Show. When
that name proved too cumbersome for 8 x 10 posters,
we shortened it to Wigglefoot.

Although I loved playing in Wigglefoot, I never
really saw myself pursuing music as a career. I would
attribute that, at least in part, to the deep respect I had
gained for music while listening to the Dead. I had
learned not to take music lightly. Which isn't to say
that music—especially Grateful Dead music—isn't fun.
Listening and dancing to Grateful Dead music accounts
for some of the most carefree, liberating, and, yes, fun,
times of my life. But I had also learned that in the
hands of skilled and creative musicians, the most basic
three-chord progression becomes an intricate weave of
music that can cover the full range of human emotion

and experience. But to reach those moments of ultimate creative expression takes dedication to mastering one's own instrument, music theory, musical history, and so forth. The same dedication to mastery goes for any art form. I simply did not have the desire to pursue playing music at that level.

In contrast, I had been seriously drawn to creative writing from the time I was sixteen. Interestingly enough, that was the same age I attended my first Dead show. The same age I sat in a room full of friends, drew a little mushroom dripping with dew on the top of a sheet of lined notebook paper, and wrote this small, fledgling poem:

I Write To You

I write for sorrow & for pain
I write for men with face nor name

I write for men with time to kill
Cause if I don't, then who will

I write for the ones with no life,
No family or friends
for Them
The suffering never ends

These are the people we see everyday
Faces without names we just pass on the way

As we go along with the games that we play
These are the ones who are new

And for them
I write to you

I certainly don't claim this poem—even as a work of juvenilia—as any sort of literary masterpiece. The contradiction in the wording of *"with* face *nor* name" is problematic enough. And that's just the start. But for a sixteen-year-old kid, high on psychedelic mushrooms, with no formal poetry education—I think it shows promise. Hell, I wasn't doing shit in my high school classes. I certainly wasn't allowed anywhere near an upper-level English class where I might've actually learned a few things about poetry.

At the very least, this poem shows a young mind ready to embrace fundamental countercultural ideals and stances. At that time, those ideals were communicated to me exclusively through the music of the 60s and its related culture. I embraced that outsider, idealist stance at the same time that I began dedicating myself to creative writing.

Plus, my writing really tripped my friends out. I mean, most of them had never heard me say anything vaguely poetic, much less commit something so deeply personal to paper and present it to the group. But that's exactly what I did with *"I Write To You,"* and continued doing through the end of high school and beyond. I was a Deadhead in love with language. The music of language. And I seemed to have a knack for using words to express ideas and emotions that my peers felt as well.

Even before I had begun any form of literary education, I firmly believed that:

1) I was a writer.
2) My artistic education would take place outside of the classroom.

In short, I knew all along that my time spent on the road with the Grateful Dead was about more than indulging my jones for other people's art. It was also informing and fueling my own art. As I rode from city to city, I kept a journal—navy blue, fastened closed with a gold button—in which I wrote my little poems. When I started hanging out with Douglas, those poems became songs as well. I wasn't reading poetry during any of this time, and I wasn't doing much revising once I wrote something down either. Every once in a while, I'd stumble across someone talking about books, or even selling their books or reciting their poems, in the parking lot at Dead shows. Although these people always got my attention, I was somehow divorced from the process of seeing my work, or even my interest in writing and literature, as formal in that way. Perhaps that sort of outward acknowledgment seemed too much "like school" for me to bother with. Outside of memorizing Hunter and Barlow lyrics, I didn't read or think about other people's poetry. I had very few models with which to compare or educate my poetry.

Frankly, I liked it that way. I freely acknowledge now that that gap in education slowed the formal side of my artistic progress—it is my main regret in rejecting the strictures of formal education. However, unbeknownst to me, I was also practicing some of the ideals set forth by legion of freethinking American literary figures—from Emerson to Whitman to the poet who took acid with Bob Weir and Phil Lesh at the very first Acid Test: Allen Ginsberg.

It would be roughly five years after I started listening to the Dead and writing poems that I would even pick up books by Ginsberg—and, more powerfully for me personally, Jack Kerouac. Much longer before I realized how influential these writers and their peers known as The Beats were on the Grateful Dead. In fact, those connections solidified around the same time my pickup truck got broken into while parked near the panhandle of Golden Gate Park and the precious blue journal I'd carried for thousands of miles was stolen.

All of my poetry from tour was in that journal.

Time to start again.

On July 26, 1990, Brent Mydland died of an overdose from a mixture of morphine and cocaine. Brent's angst and demons had always come through in his playing, resonating strongly with me and my peers. After all, we were teenagers, riddled with our own angst, searching to find our identities in the muddy middle ground between teen and adulthood. Brent had never quite fit into the Grateful Dead. He was too raw. Too young. Not intellectual enough. In Grateful Dead terms, we recognized Brent as the heir to Pigpen's boozy, blues heritage. However, the Dead had outgrown Pigpen. And perhaps the sad truth, despite the Dead band members' protestations, is that no keyboard player would ever be allowed complete acceptance as a band member after him.

In his 1991 *Rolling Stone* interview, Jerry Garcia made some lucid, honest observations about Brent and his place in the band: "Brent had this thing that he was never able to shake, which was that thing of being the new guy. And he wasn't the new guy; I mean, he was with us for ten years! That's longer than most bands even last. And we didn't treat him like the new guy. We never did that to him. It's something he did to himself. But it's true that the Grateful Dead is tough to . . . I mean, we've been together so long, and we've been through so much, that it is hard to be a new person around us.

"But Brent had a deeply self-destructive streak. And he didn't have much supporting him in terms of an intellectual life . . . . Brent was from the East Bay, which is one of those places that is like *non*culture. There's nothing there. There's no substance, no background. And Brent wasn't a reader, and he hadn't really been introduced to the world of ideas on any level. So a certain part of him was like a guy in a rat cage, running as fast as he could and not getting anywhere. He didn't have any deeper resources."

To kids growing up in the suburbs of Upstate New York, a bastion of "*non*culture," this aimless raging spoke directly to our limited life experience. Brent's singing and playing translated our sense of estrangement with the 80s culture we had grown up with into music. To us, Brent was "the man." He pushed Jerry to energetic new levels of playing while always being deferential, letting Jerry lead the way, as was only right and proper. He pushed Bobby in his vocals and injected some welcomed edginess into standbys like "Little Red Rooster," "Jack Straw," and "C. C. Rider." Brent had pushed the Dead through one of their most accomplished musical periods—the mid- to late-80s—always bringing the energy one notch higher, challenging the old boys to keep up with his licks and raspy vocals.

Unfortunately, Brent's angst and sadness wasn't just for show. It was real, and it was deadly. Jerry again:

"Brent was not a real happy person. And he wasn't like a total drug person. He was the kind of guy that went out occasionally and binged. And that's probably what killed him. Sometimes it was alcohol, and sometimes it was other stuff. When he would do that, he was one of those classic cases of a guy whose personality would change entirely, and he would just go completely out of control."

Brent's marriage to Lisa Sullivan was marked by fights; breakups; and subsequent erratic, drug-and-alcohol-fueled bad scenes. His love for his daughter was poignantly spotlighted in the song "I Will Take You Home." There is a beautiful photo of Brent's daughter Jessica sitting next to him during a show at the Shorline Amphitheatre and looking up at him while he sings that song to her; the photo becomes devastating when you realize it was taken a month before his death. Being constantly on tour and often on bad terms with his wife must have left Brent feeling guilty about being separated from her. Brent had OD'd and was resuscitated shortly before his final, fatal overdose. Between that OD and some past DUIs, he was facing jail and rehab time. So maybe he was looking for one last crazy binge before he went straight. Or maybe he was looking for a way out of all his pain and confusion.

There are many Dead episodes that come with blurry edges, but I can still vividly recall eating dinner in my parents' kitchen when the phone rang, and Sissy told me that Brent had died. We learn early that death is a part of life, but some deaths carry with them a separate, personal death of sorts to you as witness. In Brent's youthful fire, arrogance, innocence, brazenness, freedom, passion, and barely tapped potential, I had recognized those same qualities in myself. The Dead were always very upfront about the importance of the crowd's energy on their own playing—if the crowd was responsive to the music, the music would be responsive to the crowd—thus encouraging the Deadheads' investment in pumping up the band and creating good vibes on the scene. I had taken that to heart: when Brent was wailing on his keyboards and shredding the speakers with his vocals, I was right there with him. We were one. In other words, I was willing to put the majority of my creative energy into being a Deadhead and making sure the band was firing on all cylinders. Aside from the potency of his music, it was apparent to me that Brent needed that return energy the most. He was the most vulnerable, the outsider, the brilliant long shot whom I wanted to see succeed.

But when the phone rang that summer in 1990, I realized that Brent hadn't succeeded. Plain and simple: he had died. And on top of feeling a deep sadness for the waste and loss, I felt a newfound sense of responsibility. This would be a new era for the Dead. It would also be a new era for me.

So Many
Roads

In his perfectly flip manner, Bob Weir once said of Deadheads: "They seem to be enjoying themselves. If I were fresh out of school, I can't imagine anything I'd rather do than just take up and travel around, following a band I really liked."

He's got a point. This is an absolutely reasonable observation.

Fittingly enough, though, Jerry Garcia gave the most personally resonant quotes I have ever read about being a Deadhead and the gift that the Dead gave to late–twentieth-century American kids: " . . . here we are, we're getting into our fifties, and where are these people who keep coming to our shows coming from? What do they find so fascinating about these middle-aged bastards playing basically the same thing we've always played? I mean, what do seventeen-year-olds find fascinating about this? I can't believe it's just because they're interested in picking up on the Sixties, which they missed. Come on, hey, the Sixties were fun, but shit, it's fun being young, you know, nobody really misses out on that. So what is it about the Nineties in America? There must be a dearth of fun out there in America. Or adventure. Maybe that's it, maybe we're just one of the last adventures in America. I don't know."

By 1993, Garcia had crystallized the kernel of this idea into a more unified, dead-on statement: "You can't hop freights anymore but you can chase the Grateful Dead around. You can have all your tires blown out in some weird town in the Midwest and you can get hell from strangers. You can have something that lasts throughout your life as an adventure, the times you took chances. I think that's essential in anybody's life, and it's harder and harder to do in America. If we're providing some margin of that possibility, then that's great."

Even before the Dead turned into road warriors, Jerry had been influenced heavily by Jack Kerouac and the magical promise of the picaresque narrative. The transformative power of *the road*. In light of that, his stated dedication to providing an outlet for that

youthful wandering—so important to America's artistic
heritage—strikes me as a particularly selfless and
underemphasized contribution to the larger culture.

In 1964, as a banjo slinger and folk enthusiast, Jerry
and his like-minded friend Sandy Rothman hopped into
Jerry's '61 Corvair to catch shows on the bluegrass cir-
cuit. As Dennis McNally notes in his Dead biography *A
Long Strange Trip*: "The summer of 1964 was a hell of a
time for a Jew and a 'Mexican' driving a car with
California plates to go into the deep South. It was the
Freedom Summer, and the South was writhing with
change—and danger." He goes on to tell how Garcia,
"shaved his goatee and cut his hair short, and in his new
windbreaker he looked, Sara [his wife at the time]
thought, like a gas station attendant. He and Sandy
managed to traverse the South without overt incident,
but Jerry would remember it as 'creepy,' based on the
reactions they got to their license plates and 'foreign-
sounding' names."

Also predictive of the Dead times to come, they
brought along a Wollensak recorder and blank seven-
inch tapes to record the bluegrass music so that they
could listen and learn from it after the tour was over.
Together, Garcia and Rothman toured the country,
digging the smoking bluegrass music, taping shows, and
meeting like-minded music-heads. As fate would have
it, another young folkie and mandolin prodigy, David

Grisman, had started out from the East Coast on a similar mission. Garcia and Grisman met in the parking lot outside a bluegrass festival in North Carolina. Grisman and his band, the New York Ramblers, had just won the Union Grove Fiddler's Competition at the festival. Garcia told the story about meeting Grisman to John Carlini in a 1991 interview for *Guitar* magazine: "I was traveling South with Sandy Rothman, and we were recording and meeting guys in bluegrass bands. We were hungry bluegrass nuts from the West Coast, where bluegrass never finds its way. Actually, we were accompanying the Kentucky Colonels at that time in the early sixties; were part of their tour across the United States. They were ending in Boston, but we went south to Alabama and Florida, and came up through Georgia. So we'd just gotten to Pennsylvania after being on the road for three to four weeks; I got out of the car, and Grisman was walking across the parking lot with kind of a long coat on and a mandolin case. I introduced myself, and we started talking, maybe picked a few tunes or something."

That meeting would spark a friendship that lasted until Garcia's death and resulted in numerous musical collaborations over the years. Garcia's friendship with Rothman lasted the rest of his life too. In fact, it is no reach to say that Garcia's friendships and collaborations with Rothman and Grisman helped spur a resurgent

interest in roots music among American audiences in
the 1980s and 90s. When Garcia re-formed his old band
the Black Mountain Boys in 1987—featuring Rothman
on banjo—they participated in a historic eighteen-show
run of Jerry Garcia concerts at the Lunt-Fontanne
Theatre on Broadway. This success was followed by a
rekindling of Garcia's friendship with Grisman, which
resulted, among other musical gems, in the 1993 album
Not for Kids Only, a collection of roots music that has
helped pass the torch to another generation of fans.

But before the albums, the Broadway shows, and
the accolades, there were a bunch of music-loving kids
traveling the country to chase after the music they
loved, played by the musicians they admired. They were
also out there to meet like-minded people and see more
of the country. Maybe even have some adventures along
the way.

When Brent Mydland died in 1990, the Dead brought
on Vince Welnick to take over the keyboards and high
harmonies, and Bruce Hornsby became a regular guest-
performer. A new era was upon us. Unfortunately, the
scene had reached a critical mass. The popularity of
the band had skyrocketed, bringing with it gangs of
uninitiated kids who were attracted to the partying
environment more than the music. My family had
always had a reverence for the history of the band—that
respect had translated to our willingness to learn the

ways of the scene. To respect the scene. To pay attention to the words and the lessons of the old-guard hippies who had been living on the road since before we were born. Even the crazy ones—and there were many—had lessons to impart.

Some of these crazy old hippies we called "Hey Buddies" for their tendency to greet everyone with that phrase as a precursor to hitting them up for some money, a beer, a hit of your joint, some food, whatever else you had that looked appealing. "Hey buddy, give me a hit off that pipe." "Hey buddy, let me have one of those burritos." Their voices, always shot with years of alcohol abuse and smoke, crept out of their withered chests like the death rattles of grinning skeletons. They usually stank and seldom changed their clothes. I still remember Sissy and I planting ourselves next to a ragged Hey Buddy named Red on a grassy hill outside the Cal Expo while he banged a tambourine and told pretty passing girls to "put your tit in my tambourine!"

This, of course, is a totally offensive and politically incorrect thing to say. Particularly in the middle of a peace-loving scene like a Dead show. But Red had a comment for every man that walked by too. He was an equal opportunity ball-buster. And we loved it. He insulted us too, and we didn't give a damn. We thought Red was hilarious. We would roll on the ground slapping each other on the back and watching the self-righteous, shocked reactions of people who didn't know what to make of this freaky relic. Red was Red, that was all. There was no bullshit there, and he wasn't making the request out of malice or aggression. He was some sort of drunken buddha of the perfectly placed insult; an insult that could result in satori (a kick in the eye, a burst of enlightenment) for the receiver if taken correctly. If you were too offended by Red's gag come-ons—it was probably time to loosen up and stop taking yourself so damn seriously. If you laughed it off and walked on enjoying the wild spirit of all these different personalities, then perhaps you were ready to take everything as it came. As one must on the road.

As East Coast Heads, we had no problem with insults as humor. We ripped on each other all the time. And, as new kids came into the scene and we were no longer the junior Heads, we increasingly enjoyed confronting strangers and young Heads in the name of educating them on how to behave in the scene. As crazy as he was, that was Red's role too. Many of these crazy old hippies who came off so gruff were really imparting lessons on how to survive on the road and keep the scene together.

But those efforts were failing.

The scene was coming apart before our moonstruck eyes. By the early 90s, even the best efforts of Heads to police each other were coming up short. There were simply too many people around with no respect for how

to keep the scene alive. The term "gate-crasher"
became as ubiquitous as tie-dye and tofu. The Dead
were sending out missives, begging people without
tickets not to come to shows because the scene was
getting too hairy. They knew that the cops and feds
were cracking down on kids. They knew that local
stores and hotels were taking advantage of the shows to
jack up their rates. The shit was coming down. There
were too many busts and too many kids who translated
the freedom of the Dead into an increasingly aggressive
anarchic posturing. Don't have a ticket? Just "crash the
gates" and get into the show. Glass doors were smashed
in. Fences were kicked down. To our dismay, these gate-
crashers were often greeted with cheers by people who
were already inside the show. Their behavior was
celebrated as a victory over the authority figures who
were exerting more and more negative control over
the scene. The cops arrested the kids, and the kids
destroyed the venues. The venues and the media
started taking it out on the band. Deadheads were
getting a bad rap because of the people who didn't
know how to behave at shows. The whole scene was
getting out of hand.

Every time we heard about another gate-crashing or
another physical altercation between fans and the cops,
it was like someone had punched Garcia in the head.
Had punched us in the head. Every time we saw kids

lined up to pay $5 for a balloon full of nitrous sold out of
the back of a rental van by people who didn't give a fuck
about the music, only making money, it was like being
spiritually skull-fucked. Those same kids gripping their
five dollar bills, dizzy with nitrous, were the same ones
who would pass out and crack their heads on the pave-
ment, thus bringing more cops and ambulance sirens
into the environment. Bringing on the dark energy.

Deadheads were watching their world being system-
atically picked apart by assholes on every side.

And now Brent was gone.

It was around this same time—the early 90s—that
I was in school up in Potsdam. I was playing more
music on my own. I had fallen into a great scene of
musicians, artists, poets, environmentalists, and young
hippies. I didn't have the chops yet to play gigs on
guitar, so on weekends I helped set up equipment and
work the soundboard for Douglas's band Fathead Minnow. In 1991, Shasta enrolled in Potsdam and joined my
scene up there. He was a great addition to the creative
environment. Since going on tour, Shasta had become
an incredible percussionist, even studying with legendary drummer and member of the Dead family tree
Babatunde Olantunji one summer. Shasta was a fixture
in parking lot drum circles and had emerged as a leader
in that Deadhead subculture. So, naturally, when he
moved up to Potsdam, he immediately joined Fathead

Minnow, playing congas and bongos as percussive counterpoint to Douglas's creative and expressive drumming style.

Naturally, Fathead Minnow played a bunch of Dead covers. Everyone in the band was influenced by the Dead and other 60s-born bands in one way or another. Fathead Minnow extended their jams out as far as their talent and communication would allow and garnered a loyal following among students. They were keeping the spirit of improvisational rock music alive in our isolated little environment. They also played a handful of original tunes—some of which I had written the lyrics to—that complemented their cover selections. In addition to Dead tunes, Fathead Minnow started to cover songs by some newer bands too. Within our group, these newer bands were starting to crop up more and more in musical discussions and as background to our parties and smoke sessions. The three new bands that were making the strongest showing were Widespread Panic, Blues Traveler, and, most of all, Phish.

In the early 90s, Phish was just breaking out of their role as a Burlington bar-band. They had started playing shows on college campuses and at clubs and bars around the East Coast. Because of Potsdam's close proximity to Burlington and our dedication to jam-based music, we tuned into Phish's music early and with relish. On April 21, 1991, Phish was hired by our student activities committee to play a show in our student union to celebrate Earth Day. The show was free to all students. My friends and I had been listening heavily to their album *Lawnboy* as well as a handful of tapes from live shows. We had basically pestered the activities committee into booking Phish to play at the school. So by the time they arrived on campus, we were already familiar with Phish's repertoire and ready to rock out. When Phish pulled up to our student union and started unloading equipment—I was right there to help them. My strongest memory of that experience is being inside the back of the truck, unloading equipment with drummer John Fishman. I had never seen the band live, so when I asked if they needed the trampolines onstage, I didn't really expect him to say yes. But he did. Ditto the blue vacuum cleaner and an already thinning black dress with orange polka dots that, it turned out, was Fishman's gig outfit. I scratched my head, but sure enough, later on that night Fishman managed to pull off an extended vacuum cleaner solo by blowing in reverse through the nozzle while wearing the black dress with orange polka dots. Somewhere along the way, Trey Anastasio and Mike Gordon also executed a synchronized trampoline routine while they played, respectively, guitar and bass.

Mystery solved.

Once the equipment was unloaded that afternoon, my friends and I dashed out to put on our preconcert buzz. As we smoked pot, drank beer, and listened to *Lawnboy* in preparation for the show, I had the vibrant feeling of being on the cusp of something new, something burgeoning, something that was born of our own times, something we could lay claim to. It was obvious that Phish was heavily influenced by the Dead, but at the same time their sound was uniquely their own. In fact, their explorations had as much (if not more) to do with Frank Zappa and the Talking Heads as they did with the Dead. Their sound was ironic, goofy, mistrustful yet authentic, and their improvisational heights were spellbinding. Up till that point, I had never heard a live band that made me feel like the Dead's musical legacy could carry on beyond the band. Much less take off in an exciting new direction. But as my friends and I took over the student union that night, dancing across the open—acoustically horrific—auditorium while Phish blew the room apart, I saw that the future of improvisational rock-based music didn't have to be lost to scene-spoiling assholes. There were alternatives. There was a new crop of bands coming into their own across the country who would keep the music alive. They were not the Dead. But they were the next generation arriving at just the time when the Dead scene was beginning to eat itself alive.

Once Phish broke on the national scene, it was apparent that a new group of what would eventually be deemed "jam bands" was alive and kicking. In late July 1991, Sissy and I went up to a music festival, headlined by Phish, at a hippie-haven called Arrowhead Ranch in the Catskills. The festival included the Spin Doctors (who were just about to break nationally with a triple platinum album titled *Pocket Full of Kryptonite*), The Radiators, The Authority, and TR3. Phish played with a brass section called The Big Country Horns. The scene was amazing. The parking lot was filled, just like at a Dead show, but there was virtually no law enforcement on hand. People danced, dosed, partied, and came together through the music with no bullshit from outside forces. The only thing missing from the scene were the old hippies kicking everyone's asses and telling them how to behave. So that role was left up to us. We were now the senior tour-heads, and we were the ones showing the kids how to make the scene.

Between 1990 and 1995, I alternated between going to Dead shows at huge venues and checking out the new jam bands in bars and clubs. I saw Phish at least twenty times in those early days. At one gig, I saw John Popper of Blues Traveler take the stage with them at a little club in Burlington and blow the crowd's mind with an a capella percussive mouth jam. I also went to shows and saw Widespread Panic, the Spin Doctors,

The Radiators, the Aquarium Rescue Unit, and a whole host of regionally based bands who were making their own scenes, their own environment, outside of the mainstream. The music was stellar, and the musicians were right there—you could talk to them, meet them, stand in front of the stage and watch their chops. Tickets were only ten bucks, sometimes less. Sometimes, as with my first Phish concert at Potsdam and another Phish show a year later (May 12, 1992) at St. Lawrence University, the shows were even free.

The more I was able to access great improvisational music on a smaller, hassle-free scale, the less I was inclined to put up with the obstacles that came along with going to Dead shows. Frankly, the musical highs I had heard the Dead hit in the late 80s—widely acknowledged as some of the best in the band's history—were fewer and farther between too. The band had lost a lot of power when Brent died, and it was taking them time to pull it back together again. Don't get me wrong, when the band was clicking, no new-jack jam band could touch them. They were still the Dead. The drains on the scene had tapped a lot of positive energy from shows, though, and that loss of energy translated to the band's music as well.

In the summer of 1995, I was three years out of Potsdam. I had been spending my time traveling the country in a blue Ford Ranger with a cap on the back covering a futon mattress. That was my portable bedroom. I crisscrossed the country, staying with friends and basically roaming without a plan. I spent a lot of time out in San Francisco hanging out with Jay and a bunch of the Allegheny crew who had moved out there after graduation. At one point, a friend and I drove the Ranger down to the tip of the Baja Peninsula, camping out and having adventures along the way. We did the same thing through Europe. I settled into a sort of routine, going on the road and then living for a few months in Boulder, Colorado, during spring and summer; working some shit job; seeing bands at the Fox Theatre; and partying with Rochester friends and friends-of-friends who had moved out there. Then, for a few months in fall and winter, I would go live with Karen. She had been accepted into a PhD program for clinical psychology at the University of Missouri–St. Louis (UMSL) and was living in a one-bedroom apartment in St. Louis. We had been through a lot together in the ten years of our on-and-off–again relationship, and—though she had her shit together and was pursuing her professional ambition—she was willing to help me out while I wandered. I stayed at her apartment rent free. I worked as a delivery man bringing orders of flowers and pharmaceuticals to hospitals and retirement homes. For a while, I worked as a disc jockey at weddings and parties. Unfortunately, my musical background brought nothing to the table when it came to working hick VFW weddings and kid parties around Missouri and Illinois. I was, in fact, a horrible DJ.

It was during this period that my true education as a writer began. Despite outward appearances, that was actually the purpose of this entire period. I was traveling, meeting new people outside the bubble of the Dead universe, and reading ferociously. Every time I went to St. Louis, I wrote a new novel manuscript and dozens of poems and stories. Karen's enrollment at UMSL also gave me access to the university's library. Every week, I checked out stacks of books, devouring everyone from Dostoyevsky, Tolstoy, and Celine to Bukowski, Henry Miller, and the Marquis de Sade. I read constantly and worked hard at becoming a better writer. Most of my writing was a flop, but this period also brought my first publications—weird little stories and poems that appeared in stapled zines put together by obsessive editors working out of small, dimly lit rooms around the country. Each time one of these publications—with names like *The Basement Magazine*, *Driver's Side Airbag*, and *Alpha Beat Soup*—arrived, I was buoyed up by a sense of accomplishment.

In one sense, I was doing it. I was becoming a writer.

In another sense, I was broke. Getting depressed about the future. Leeching off my girlfriend. Making no motions toward a sustainable adulthood.

By the time the Dead played St. Louis in the summer
of 1995, their tour had already been stricken with
problems. This summer tour is often referred to as "the
cursed tour." By this time, camping and vending at
venue parking lots had basically been banned as a way
of dealing with the problems the scene had experienced. Despite the band's request that this ban be
honored, the town of Highgate, Vermont—with dollar
signs in their eyes—allowed camping and vending
adjacent to the show site. This was the first stop on the
East Coast summer tour, and 20,000 people without
tickets descended on the town. Recognizing that the
scene would quickly go bad if these masses were denied
entry to the show, the gates were thrown open and
everyone was allowed entry.

Less than two weeks later, three fans were struck by
lightning in the parking lot outside a show in Washington, D.C.

The scene was dissolving fast and, as if they were
symbiotically linked organisms, Jerry had relapsed and
sunk deeper into heroin addiction and exhaustion. His
playing was uninspired, even disoriented, and inside
the band there was talk about the need to intervene.
Never the Dead's strong suit.

In Noblesville, Indiana, at a venue that used to be
called Deer Creek but now operates under a corporate
moniker like so many venues across the nation, a death

threat was made on Jerry's life before the first show.
The band seriously debated not playing at all. In the
end, the show went on, but only with metal detectors
installed at the gates, heavy police presence, and the
house lights on throughout the show. As if this wasn't
bad enough, the venue was again overrun by people
coming to the show without tickets. Rather than peace-
fully accepting their lot and making the best of it in the
parking lot outside the show, these fuckers kicked holes
into the fences surrounding the venue and flooded in.
The band was scheduled to play the next night, but
after the debacle of the gate-crashers the night before—
including, to the horror of the band, the cheers from the
audience that the crashers' idiocy had brought on—the
local police told the venue that they would not provide
security for the second gig.

In a sense, the anarchy of the new Dead fans had
won. They'd forced the authorities out of the scene.

But, by law, without security, you can't have a concert.

The second gig was canceled.

It was the first time in thirty years that the behavior
of the fans had caused the band to cancel a show.

It is a sign of how jaded (and broke) I had become,
that I didn't even bother going to see the Dead when
the band rolled into St. Louis that summer. All reports
confirmed that the band's playing was off, and the scene
was horrible. Although it had nothing to do with the
show directly, my judgment felt sadly confirmed when

I watched the news reports about the show that night.
The scene looked like a poorly acted recreation of a
Dead show. A Dead show as portrayed by the Lifetime
Channel. At a campground filled with fans, twenty
miles away from the concert venue, a porch roof had
collapsed, sending 108 people to the hospital. One man
was paralyzed.

The "cursed tour" ended on July 9 at Soldier Field in
Chicago.

That was to be the Grateful Dead's last show.

One month later, Jerry Garcia was dead. He had
checked himself into a rehab clinic called Serenity
Knolls in Marin County, California, on the evening of
August 8. By 4:23 A.M. the next morning, he was found
dead in his bed of a heart attack.

Obviously, my Dead touring days were done before
Jerry's death. I had moved into a new phase, practicing
my own creativity, traveling the country, and soaking in
the new jam scene. I was working toward becoming a
writer, and all my efforts were directed at that cause.

Yet I always realized that I wouldn't have reached
that point in my own development without my experiences with the Grateful Dead. I was struggling and
depressed, but I also had the emboldening belief that
I was on the road to something better. To my own
creative fulfillment. Without my experiences as a
Deadhead, I wouldn't have known the possibilities of a
full-time creative existence. I wouldn't have known the

power of an alternative point of view. I wouldn't have known how to travel and meet strange new people in new places. I wouldn't have believed in—or experienced to such a life-altering extent—the transformative power of art.

I wouldn't be who I was.

Jerry's death hit me with a sadness that took me off-guard. Perhaps I had kidded myself that I was beyond caring about the band in such a deep way. I had moved on. I was fulfilling my own creative process now. I had outgrown my obsession with the band and its members. But that wasn't true. Jerry wasn't just a member of the Grateful Dead. In many ways, he was the most important teacher I had ever had.

I cried when Jerry died like I hadn't cried in years. Like I cried when any close friend or family member had died. I had already mourned the loss of the Dead scene that had enriched my life. Somehow, though, I had never given up the possibility that I could go back there. That eventually, the scene would settle down and I could return there for a little bit longer. Maybe a lot longer.

But when Jerry died, that possibility was gone too. There would be no going back. The loss this time was not just figurative, but literal. The Grateful Dead were gone.

Jerry was gone.

We were on our own.

Chapter Sixteen

Wake of
the Flood

Bill Monroe—one of Jerry's bluegrass idols—once
said that his audience was "people who get up every
morning and make biscuits."

Jerry Garcia could easily have said that his audience
was "people who get up every afternoon and take
bong hits."

It would've gotten a good laugh (something Jerry
knew how to appreciate), but it wouldn't have been
true. In typical Garcia fashion, he spoke of the Dead's
relationship to their audience in much more cosmic
terms. "I was thinking about the Grateful Dead and
their success. And I thought that maybe this idea of a

transforming principle has something to do with it. Because when we get onstage, what we really want to happen is, we want to be transformed from ordinary players into extraordinary ones, like forces of a larger consciousness. And the audience wants to be transformed from whatever ordinary reality they may be in to something a little wider, something that enlarges them. So maybe that's the notion of transformation, a seat-of-the-pants shamanism, that has something to do with why the Grateful Dead keep pulling them in. Maybe that's what keeps the audience coming back and what keeps it fascinating for us, too."

Never was the importance of the Dead—the diversity of their influence and the depth of their fan base—as apparent as when Jerry Garcia died.

Fittingly, San Francisco mayor Frank Jordan flew a tie-dyed flag at half mast over City Hall to commemorate his passing. Perhaps surprisingly ("I never inhaled"), perhaps not, President Bill Clinton also acknowledged the loss with sympathetic remarks. Of course, famous musicians and celebrities had their remarks noted and recorded for the public record. Bob Dylan said of Garcia, "He is the very spirit personified of whatever is muddy river country at its core and screams up into the spheres. He really had no equal . . . . There are a lot of spaces and advances between the Carter Family, Buddy Holly, and, say, Ornette Coleman, a lot of universes, but he filled them all without being a member of any school. His playing was moody, awesome, sophisticated, hypnotic and subtle."

Master African drummer Babatunde Olantunji, who led the funeral drum procession for the 25,000 mourners who showed up at the memorial gathering for Jerry on August 13, 1995, in Golden Gate Park, fittingly, simply bid farewell to "our friend, Jerry Garcia."

But the majority of us, the nonfamous and nonconnected, the Deadheads and the fans across the world, came together in groups to honor Jerry's legacy in our own way. We talked about shows and relived our fondest memories of Jerry's guitar-work and his uncanny ability to inhabit the roles of the characters he sang about. We passed joints and looked at pictures of the man on and off stage. We wondered about what this meant for the future of the band—all the while knowing, but not wanting to say out loud, that the Grateful Dead were through.

But, mainly, we did what Jerry would've wanted us to do. We came together and played his music. Loud.

I was living in St. Louis when Jerry died. I had never been there long enough to make any new friends, so I made phone calls instead. I regretted not going to see the band at one of their last gigs in St. Louis, but only in a historical sense. One last time to see Jerry onstage. This was before the time when the Internet was omnipresent in every household, so all the information I got was through friends on the phone and waiting for twenty-second reports on the news. There were not the dozens of networking sites buzzing with information as there would be now. We talked to each other. We wrote letters and shared our memories. And we listened to the music.

Karen and I were going through a rocky period. My seeming aimlessness was contrasting more and more with her professional focus. Plus, St. Louis was her city. She had new friends there and was pursuing a new life. At that moment, I was feeling more and more like a relic from her past. At gatherings with her fellow PhD students, I was a long-haired, scruffy, stoned hippie in the midst of clean-cut, overachieving budding-psychologists. They were sipping wine and talking about their courses, professors, internships, and job prospects. I was trying to write books that no one seemed very interested in reading.

Frankly, I was feeling like a relic from my own history as well. I was divorced from the Dead scene that helped put me on the road. I was out of touch with Shasta and Sissy and many other family members. I was geographically isolated from my closest friends, and all my family were back East. I was writing every day, but each rejection slip from a prospective literary agent or publisher pushed me deeper into an understanding that

I wouldn't be making my living as a writer anytime
soon. The future was bleak. My novels weren't selling,
and the strange little zines I was publishing in weren't
going to cut it in the long haul.

I was already in the throes of depression when Jerry
died. I knew something had to change, but I was stuck.
I was alienated from my surroundings. Now my girlfriend didn't want to deal with me anymore either.
I could feel the connection draining away, and my
sadness only pushed us farther apart. I couldn't sleep,
and she couldn't be expected to comfort an adult man
sobbing at 3:00 A.M. every night. She got up in the
morning to go to class. I smoked cigarettes on the back
fire escape and sat at the little wooden kitchen table
in the shotgun apartment trying to write books.

And now Jerry was gone. And my last out—going
back on the road with the Grateful Dead—was gone
with him.

I knew that I'd have to split St. Louis. For the
moment, my romantic relationship with Karen was
basically over. But the idea of simply hopping into the
truck and taking off again with no plan in mind now
paralyzed me with fear. One of my poet friends from
back in Potsdam was enrolled in an MFA program for
poetry at Colorado State in Ft. Collins. He loved it and
urged me to try an MFA program myself. But there
were problems with that as well. My college grades

had been shit. I had never taken a GRE and—having been diagnosed with a learning disability back in college—I knew that, even if I took the test, my score would only hurt my chances. Plus, I had no way of accounting for how I had spent the past three years other than the fact that I'd been wandering the country and writing.

There was only one place that seemed like a possibility. Douglas had gone to the Naropa Institute and loved it there. As it turned out, they offered an MFA degree in creative writing. Better yet, their program was called The Jack Kerouac School of Disembodied Poetics. And the coup de grâce—they didn't require GRE scores and based their acceptance solely on the applicant's writing and application essay.

I filled out the MFA application and put together the required number of sample writing pages. That part was easy, I'd written three novels and dozens of stories and poems by that point. Finally, I sat down at the little wooden kitchen table and wrote my essay, telling the Naropa faculty what I had been up to. I didn't try to dress it up at all. I'd been driving around the country, writing, and working shitty jobs. That was it. At that time, Naropa was the one MFA program that would've actually regarded that path, the past three years of my life, as time well spent. Naropa's writing program was founded by Allen Ginsberg and poet Anne Waldman in

1974 as a place to blend contemplative practice (namely, Buddhism) with creative writing. On the school's website, Waldman explains that the school was called "Disembodied" because "so many of our faculty would be peripatetic, and also our inspiration was from many writers long gone. Moreover, at the time we had no buildings, no desks, no blackboards, no filing cabinets, no grades, no money . . . only our mental commitment, our voices, our scholarship, our practice. So in the beginning, the school was truly disembodied!" Ginsberg said of the original intent of the Jack Kerouac School of Disembodied Poetics: "It would be a way of teaching meditators about the golden mouth and educating poets about the golden mind."

Yes, Jerry was gone, but Ginsberg, the man and the guiding spirit—the poet who had sat tripping with the boys in the band at the very first Acid Test—was still around. So if the spirit of the road and the counter-culture was alive at Naropa—that's where I would go.

I was accepted into Naropa's MFA program in Writing & Poetics for the fall 1995 semester. I packed my laptop computer, my guitar and amp, my bag full of clothes, and my futon mattress into the back of my Ford Ranger.

I didn't know that Karen and I would reconcile nearly two years later. That once we had gained more control over our own lives, we would be drawn back together so strongly. That eventually we would marry and start a family together.

I didn't know that I would last only one semester at Naropa before dropping out to return back East. That I would enroll in—and eventually complete—a master's of education program at Nazareth College.

All I knew was that I was headed for a new adventure. I was pursuing my own creativity by reconnecting with the traditions that I knew were my own: the counterculture that had spawned the writing I loved best and the music that changed my life.

I was back on the road. On the bus.

I put a bootleg into the tape player and turned it up loud.

We Will
Survive

*You are thirty-seven years old. You live with your wife
and three children in a modest, well-maintained house
on the outskirts of the town you grew up in. You have a
mortgage. You have a water bill and property taxes. You
have teacher conferences, baseball practices, swimming
lessons, a nightly routine for putting the kids to bed. You
write poetry and fiction that is published in small magazines and short-run book editions that only a handful of
people ever read. You work for a small nonprofit literary
publisher in an office with large windows and a door that
you can close if you want to. Jerry Garcia is dead, and the
Grateful Dead have been gone for more than ten years*

now. You still listen to the Grateful Dead or a side-project of one of the band members almost every day. You are listening to Legion of Mary, Volume 1 of the Jerry Garcia Collection right now. Instead of that brown, vinyl briefcase covered with Dead stickers and stuffed full of coveted bootleg tapes, you now have stacks of shows burned onto CD. You also have many of the official live concert releases. You can afford to splurge on those here and there. You can also go online and download shows off different Internet websites whenever you feel like it. You no longer have to pretend to like the pretentious assholes you had to kiss up to in order to get soundboard-quality bootlegs when you were a kid. Now, it's all at your fingertips twenty-four hours a day. The hippie bureaucracy is gone.

This democratizing turn of fortunes is extremely satisfying.

You are not a kid anymore. Your hair is cropped short and shot through with gray. Your lithe, wiry dancing frame has filled out into a substantial man's body. You don't look like a Deadhead anymore. You don't own any Grateful Dead T-shirts. There are no stickers on your car. Your bracelets and necklaces have long since disintegrated. Your bag of ticket stubs lies buried beneath brown socks in a bedroom drawer. The Grateful Dead almost never come up in casual conversation. You've discovered the hard way that it's best not to talk to civilians about your touring days. The questions that come out of those admissions are never the right ones. They're never in "celebration of." They never look you straight in the eye with sympathetic interest. They never get it.

The cynicism with which many people view the Grateful Dead never ceases to take you off-guard.

You have decided this is just as well.

You never talk about your first romantic love in casual conversation either. Why would you? That first love is a highly personal matter. Despite the strains of music seeping out from under your door at work, the Grateful Dead have become a highly personal matter as well. A part of your soul that you keep private lest some cretin chip away at it.

It's none of their fucking business anyway.

Yet when you listen to this music, you still feel the same physical, spiritual, and intellectual charge you did when you were a teenager. You are just as sonically engaged as the days when touring and keeping up with the Dead was a daily fact of life. When touring and keeping up with the Grateful Dead was your life. But it isn't anymore. It's not even an option. And sometimes you wonder how this can be.

Yet there are times when you are not so alone in your love. There are times when the old enthusiasms are allowed to bubble up in a volcano of devotee gushing. You are away from your wife and family. You are on your own. You are in a bar. There is a collection of equally middle-aged Deadheads on a small stage set just far enough back from the bar and tables to allow room for the servers to get through with baskets of chicken fingers and greasy, oversized hamburgers. They are plugging in their guitars, unpacking their keyboards, and setting up the PA. Some are wearing tie-dyes. Some look like they just came from a proper family picnic. It really doesn't matter.

They look like your insurance guy. Your kid's teacher. Your trusted mechanic. Your bank teller, your computer technician, the restaurant owner with a twinkle in his eye.

And they are.

That is exactly what they are.

You stand in a corner watching the band prepare to play. You are holding your third beer in a plastic cup in front of you at mid-chest. You shift your feet back and forth because you are alone in a public place, but at the moment this is exactly where you want to be. You are not dressed for a night out. You came in whatever you happened to be wearing when you walked out the door. Jeans, sneakers, some plain earth-tone shirt—who cares?

The place smells like fried food and spilled booze. There is a distant click of pool balls. There is the laughter of the rode-hard bartender and the divorcées trying to recapture more than they should. Cigarette smoke drifts in through the door that opens onto a back patio. There is a stoned bouncer in a blue wool hat with one eye on the baseball playoffs. The Red Sox are winning. The bar is three miles down the street from your modest, well-maintained home. The home where your wife and children are now safely asleep. The home where your back deck needs to be stained again. The home where the dehumidifier in the basement just crapped out and needs to be replaced. The home you will return to eventually. At the end of the night.

But not just yet.

Your old friends start drifting into the room. The calls have gone around that a Dead cover band is playing in your little townie bar. You are happy to see these people. You grew up with them. You have known them your whole life. You still live in the same town, and you still talk to them regularly. They have jobs too. They have children and taxes and responsibilities. You realize now that no one's life is fully revealed to each other, but that doesn't matter—these people will always be your family. Why do they do what they do? Who did they end up being? Who are the bosses that they deal with, the customers that they appease, the wives and in-laws that they placate?

You know these people. They make decisions every day that you will never know about. That you would not make. That you will never understand. But, in the end, that doesn't matter either. These wheels were set in motion many years ago. You have been through too much together—too many good times and too many hard—and these are the people who are inextricably woven into the story of your life.

You loved the Dead with them. You can talk about that here. Remember. Reminisce. You freaked out together on acid. You stood side-by-side moon-eyed and trembling at the curtain of the stage while the coliseum filled up around you. You sent in your mail orders together. You traveled hundreds of miles. You linked arms in strange auditoriums and swung each other around to the stomp of "Tennessee Jed." You had shit-eating grins. These people gave you your first bootlegs. Your first hit of pot. Your first dose. They stole your first girlfriend, and though you will always remember that, you will always love them. Because life would be less without these people in it. You would be less. And one day, no one will remember that you were ever here at all.

You've finished your third beer and are on to your fourth. The band is assembling on the stage. There is no sense pretending that this is Jerry, Bob, Phil, Brent, Mickey, and Bill. You won't carry the delusion that far. This is not Alpine Valley. This is not Shoreline or Frost Amphitheater or the legendary Fillmore East. Not Freedom Hall. None of those mythical destinations that have seeded themselves into your consciousness even though you never walked through many of their doors.

You have been to them all in your ears. In your mind.
They, too, are a part of your history.

No, this is only a small, cheap bar at the four-corners
of a sorry little town. It is nowhere at all. It is what it is.

The band members look at each other and nod. They
exchange knowing glances. The drummer is grinning
widely and tapping his snare with his index finger. The
keyboardist winks at his wife and takes one last swig of
his beer. The lead guitar player steps down onto a pedal
and tremolo-laden notes issue forth from his Fender amp.
A saxophone player will sit in a little later on in the night.
But for now, it is just the basics: guitars, keyboard, drums,
and bass. The core of the music. The essence of the sound.

The drummer clicks his sticks three times to count the
band in. With a rush of sound, the first set begins with a
surging cover of "China Cat Sunflower." You start to
move. You can't help it. Your friends are moving too.
Their bodies are as bulky as yours. As laden with years,
miles, and the histories worn on their faces and strung
thick across their fleshy abdomens. We have forgotten
how to move. But we are starting to remember. You take
another pull on your beer, feeling the alcohol in your
bloodstream lubricating your motions. This is good. This
is what you need. It takes a little more lubrication these
days to get you past your days. It takes a little more to get
beyond. But you will get there. The music is playing. And
this is the time to do it. You look around at your friends

shaking their limbs and smiling widely, and you realize that, after all this time, the Dead have circled back to Magoo's Pizza Parlor. This is where it all began. The music has been liberated from the projection screens and glaring lights of the main stage that it evolved into along the way. There are no such frills here. Only the notes, the lyrics, and the songs.

The music is back where it belongs.

The music is with us.

ACKNOWLEDGMENTS

First of all, thank you to the Grateful Dead and extended family. Without you, no us. Thank you to my parents and to my entire family for their unflagging support. Thank you to my supportive and enthusiastic editor, Ben Schafer, and the hardworking crew at Da Capo Press. Thank you to my agent, Linda Roghaar, of the Linda Roghaar Literary Agency, for her guidance and advice. Thank you to Zach Hraber of Zap Solutions for my websites and Steve Smock and Chris Reeg of prime8media for the book trailer. Thank you to all who shared their passion and memories about the Grateful Dead during the writing of this book, especially Stephen Kennedy Robinson and David Scott Crissey.

To my wife, Karen, who has always believed, and to my children, who constantly bring the magic: I love you.

BIBLIOGRAPHY

Adams, Rebecca G. "Stigma and the Inappropriately Stereotyped: The Deadhead Professional." *Sociation Today, The Official Journal of The North Carolina Sociological Association* 1, no. 1 (Spring 2003), available at http://www.ncsociology.org/sociationtoday/deadhead.htm.

Berry, Paul. *On the Bus: The Complete Guide to the Legendary Trip of Ken Kesey and The Merry Pranksters and The Birth of the Counterculture.* New York: Thunder's Mouth Press, 1996.

Brandelius, Jerilyn Lee. *Grateful Dead Family Album.* New York: Warner Books, 1989.

Hencke, James. "Jerry Garcia." *Rolling Stone,* October 31, 1991.

Layden, Joe, and Steve Parish. *Home Before Daylight: My Life on the Road with the Grateful Dead.* New York: St. Martin's Press, 2003.

Lesh, Phil. *Searching for the Sound: My Life with the Grateful Dead.* New York: Little, Brown, 2005.

Levin, Daniel J. *This Is Your Brain on Music: The Science of Human Obsession.* New York: Plume, 2007.

McNally, Dennis. *Long Strange Trip: The Inside History of the Grateful Dead.* New York: Broadway, 2003.

Reich, Charles, and Jann Wenner. *Garcia: A Signpost to New Space*. San Francisco: Straight Arrow Books, 1972.

Shenk, David, and Steve Silberman. *Skeleton Key: A Dictionary for Deadheads*. New York: Main Street Books, 1994.

Trager, Oliver. *The American Book of the Dead: The Definitive Grateful Dead Encyclopedia*. New York: Fireside, 1997.

3 1901 04561 2084